POINTLESS TRAINING

The Consequences of Inadequate Training Strategies

James K. Hopkins

authorHOUSE®

AuthorHouse™
1663 Liberty Drive
Bloomington, IN 47403
www.authorhouse.com
Phone: 1 (800) 839-8640

Published by AuthorHouse 09/08/2015

ISBN: 978-1-5049-2339-2 (sc)
ISBN: 978-1-5049-3390-2 (e)

Library of Congress Control Number: 2015914003

Print information available on the last page.

Dedication

To every single person I have talked to for the past 25 years that has complained about a training event they attended and thought it was pointless and a waste of time. I heard you. I feel your pain. Whenever I have implemented training I have made it as purposeful as possible. My hope is that training professionals that want to avoid pointless training will find this book a resource and give them purpose.

Contents

Acknowledgments

Here's to the training professionals that have inspired me to take my work seriously and to build purposeful training solutions. Their ideals, programs and methodologies have produced some of the best training solutions in the market.

In alphabetical order:

Jeanette Marie Bassi

Ken Blanchard

Cynthia Clay

Stephen R. Covey

Randy Delisle

Nancy Duling

Joe Folkman

Nancy Friedman

Gary Hill

Toni Johnson

Donald Kirkpatrick

John Maxwell

Bob Pike

Hyrum Smith

Colleen VanDyke

Diane Williams

Jack Zenger

Foreword

As an employee of several companies that have not given the training function a lot of attention, and thus produced events I struggled to find relevant to my job, I applaud the passion and purpose in this attempt to push training personnel to do more than they have been doing.

For the same 25 years that Jim Hopkins has been in the training profession, I have watched and listened to him as he works to achieve purpose in his work. As his wife, I have heard about every great moment in training as well as every disappointment. His passion for trying to help as many people as he can, take this profession seriously, and do right by employees and the company that employs them, is inspiring.

I am one of the employees that he has listened to comment that a training course was a waste of my time. I've often said that the training was pointless too, so as I read these pages I couldn't help but see the times that I experienced both the right and wrong way of training, and why I hope people can be open to changing the way they do business.

As an employee that is not involved in training, I can attest to the times good training made a difference, and when poor training made my job harder than necessary.

So read every page, take good notes, and train with a purpose!

-   Lori Hopkins

Introduction

Have you ever walked out of a training workshop, a webinar or even after completing an eLearning course and said to yourself, that was a waste of time or pointless? All too often employees are being forced to participate in training that not only do they feel is pointless, but it really was unnecessary for them to attend. Maybe they already had the skills. Maybe it lacked what they really needed to know. Maybe they just didn't see the purpose. For whatever reason, the time and expense it took to develop and attend this event was pointless to them and probably pointless period.

All company executives, not just the Human Resources Director and the Training Director, should be asking these questions. Is your training a series of pointless events? What do employees say about your training efforts? Do they long for more information, different skills or a more engaging environment for learning?

While we never set out to develop pointless training solutions, pointless workshops or an entire pointless training department, it sadly happens way too often. And each time it does happen, it makes a turnaround that much harder to implement.

This book discusses the big skill areas that most companies should be developing in their employees and how to make a purposeful impact and avoid pointless processes. You no doubt will recognize times you have experienced or implemented pointless training yourself. But while recognizing pointless training is step one, the real learning comes from understanding what you can do differently going forward.

In my first book, The Training Physical™: *Diagnose, Treat and Cure Your Training Department*, I explored what it takes to have and maintain a healthy training function. In this book I continue my training philosophy using similar medical analogies at times to draw the reader into a quick understanding of how to engage learning and where employees are applauding the training function, learning applicable skills and increasing the effectiveness of the company. Like a bandage on a cut, it has its purpose when used appropriately. But when the cut needs stitches, it is pointless to use a bandage.

If you are ready to develop purposeful training solutions and avoid pointless training, then let's begin the conversation. Whether it is a book, a blog, or an article, I write as if I am talking directly to you, the reader. And although I attempt to always be polite, you may at times be offended with my blunt tone. I believe that being honest and speaking directly is my best way of getting your attention. I am not helping you at all if I play word games and you miss learning the truth.

Full Non-Disclosure:

My examples for pointless training come from clients and companies I have consulted with, but I never name names. And, unless I have witnessed a process several times I have not used it as an example in this book. When I reference "a company" it is for grammatical reasons, not to focus on a single event or company. When I reference "a bank" I am talking about an industry I have supported for 36 years, and have found to be institutions that share a lot in common. For the sake of examples, every reader has interacted with a bank so it requires a lot less background to set the stage of the learning point I am trying to make. For positive examples, unless I note otherwise, I am usually talking about a single star player or star company. However, I will still not disclose names.

Now my personal examples are for the full view of all readers. I still won't name the company, but I am the training example, so good, bad or ugly if my experiences can help others learn, I have no problem letting others know I am human and have made my share of mistakes too.

I've spent over 25 years in the learning field, and my number one objective is and always will be that the learner learns. If you are ready to learn, let's get started!

- *Jim Hopkins*

Chapter One
WHAT MAKES TRAINING POINTLESS?

Anytime that training fails to build the targeted skill it becomes a pointless activity. Anytime that a participant feels that a training event was a waste of their time it became a pointless activity for that employee. The art of designing training solutions so they are always purposeful and never pointless is an ongoing challenge for everyone involved. The secret is remaining focused on the learner while meeting the objectives of the company.

Employee Disconnect

One of my favorite authors and speakers was Stephen Covey, who wrote in **"The Seven Habits of Highly Successful People"** that we should *"Begin with the End in Mind."* It has always been one of those phrases that bonded with me from the first time I read it, and has especially stuck with me when designing training solutions.

Another thing I learned early in my training development career was to make sure I understood the purpose of training. It is the process in which we build skills in order to perform a function. The often used description of education is something entirely different from the objective of training. Education is learning about something and Training is taking that knowledge and applying it to work. I can know all about how to do something, but it is seldom beneficial to my employment if I cannot take that knowledge and perform a function.

All of the training staff, and that includes the trainer, the instructional designer, the performance consultant and the manager, must be able to zero in on both of these concepts, and then constantly assess if they are designing solutions that make the connection. When I ask a client what must the employee be able to do when we are finished with training that they cannot do now, I am targeting both of these areas. Training can easily become disconnected for the company and the employee if we fail to make it applicable and relevant.

A Pointless Training Example:

Training for the sake of training is pointless, and yet it happens. A bank comes to mind that developed several workshops in preparation for an acquisition of another bank. This training was only for the new bank's employees and the purpose was to integrate and prepare them for day one of the merger. One would think that they would have created a list of everything these employees <u>should be able to do</u> on day one, and then decide what these new employees needed training on. Well, that is not what happened.

They did develop a list of what they thought were the most important topics, and designed several workshops. What seemed to slip past this training function was any kind of audience or situational analysis, like the most obvious of facts that they would be training <u>existing bankers</u>. In this one example, they managed to achieve the top four reasons for disconnected training.

1.   Training skills that already exist
2.   Training skills that are disconnected to the purpose/objective
3.   Providing skills that are too little and too late for when needed
4.   Providing skills that are at the wrong level, either too high or too low

The all too often feedback from participants was that the training was pointless. They wanted to be prepared to function as stand-alone offices on day one of the acquisition. However, the workshops were chock full of content that these existing bankers already knew how to do. They were absent of, or they minimally targeted, the areas that needed to be developed. The main processes and the operational systems were missing, along with enough practice to build any level of competency. The skills being taught were entry level for all employees and too basic.

Training caught a break when the acquisition was delayed, and they attempted to fix the training. But at this point there was not enough time to prepare everyone and allow for the practice time to develop the skills. Although the second round was much more effective it was a little too late to make a difference.

The first few months of this new merged bank was rough on employees and customers. Training was catching none of the blame, when in fact they could have prevented a lot of the problems. The major issues that occurred were not all attributable to a lack of skills, but rather operational and procedural problems. But if the training had been designed correctly and the goals for training had been the focus, the design process would have caught many of the issues before day one. Changes in policy and procedure would have been made and problems would have been prevented. The problem is no one knew about these challenges in a training environment, but instead learned them live and in person in front of the customer.

The moral of this example should be not only that training didn't prepare employees to perform their jobs, their incompetence in the training function made other problems stay hidden until it was too late to make a difference. In this example, the training provided was pointless and the training department became pointless too. But what is scarier to me is this example is not unique. I have seen it a dozen times! Something as obvious as a merger, acquisition should prompt better training and yet over and over again the same course of events get played out. Not because it is a good business process, but rather a set of common competencies are missing in a lot of training functions and personnel.

I often am impressed by the amount of education and training that a doctor must go through before they are allowed to practice medicine by themselves. The number of years of college is then followed by a number of years of residency (practice). It is by shear experience and the number of cases they work on that builds their competencies.

I have a friend that became an RN but chose to spend her residency period in a Las Vegas Emergency Room to increase the number of experiences she would have during the same amount of time on the job at other local hospitals where she lived. The amusing side of this story is she was once a training manager that I hired years ago and my constant harping on "practice is what builds skills" sunk in with her. She told me she deliberately chose a busy hospital because she wanted a lot of practice to be the best she could be.

Unsupported Efforts

Another common theme of pointless training is in the area of support; both by the employee receiving the training and the company. Great training functions are the ones that focus on the complete learning process and support the employee with various tools. They are also the ones that understand the value of marketing the purpose of a robust learning environment by everyone involved.

Even the best designed and job connected training can bomb big time if the learner fails to connect the dots as to why they need to learn what is being trained. Adult learners need to see and feel a connection to learning something new. They must also see that the effort to learn will be put to use, and rather immediately, otherwise they will not fully engage and may even just completely tune out.

The three areas that are most common to a lack of support for training are:

1.   Not supported by the organization and/or management team
2.   Not seen as valuable by the employee themselves
3.   Not seen as applicable to a function or career path

Let's begin by agreeing that the company must benefit from every training effort because they are paying for all of it. Training is a support system for the company to achieve business objectives, so never ever implement training where the company and the applicable management members are not in agreement before things go forward. The company is the benefactor, and the management teams are the supporters, coaches, cheerleaders and as just stated, the check writers. You need them all to be on board before you set sail.

When you begin to market to employees, the true test of purposeful training becomes in how well your solution is embraced. When employees see that there are reasons and benefits to learning, you have hit your target. Trainers also realize that half the battle to training a skill is having a desire to obtain the skill. Yet we too often wait to sell training in our opening remarks for the event. This is rarely enough time for people to digest the information, and it can create a pointless event if participants don't buy in before the event has concluded.

Always answer their most common concerns when training is announced or scheduled, and again in your opening remarks.

- What will I learn?
- Why do I want to learn it?
- When will I use these skills?
- Make sure you answer: What's in it for me? (WIIFM)

When training is seen as something that is not connected to a function or career path, it may not be for a lack of marketing. It may be that it really is off the wall and completely lacking in a connection. Training should never be afraid to seek feedback of a designed solution by the very people that

11

are going to get training. Yet if we fail to pre sell employees on what and why they are about to attend training, we lose valuable early engagement that can have employees arriving to an event eager to learn. But just because we are excited about a possible training solution and can sell sand to someone living in the desert, doesn't mean we should.

Trainers sometimes get so excited about a new topic or energized by a speaker or book that they will run straight into a brick wall trying to implement the training. They never bother to connect it back to their company and the mission their company is working to achieve.

I've gone to conferences, and been so amped up after listening to a particular speaker that although the program is well designed and will achieve the targeted learning objectives, at the end of the day it is not a skill that my company will need or has a desire to develop. If there is no connection to the current or future job role, then this is not the time or place to provide the training. If I insist on implementing it, then it becomes pointless training.

This is why we must first only provide training that fits the needs of our company. Then we must sell everyone on the reasons we want to learn the skills before they enter the event.

Weak Training Solutions

If there was one thing I learned from writing my first book, ***The Training Physical*™**, it was to connect new concepts to things people already know well. The Training Physical™ is really an audit of the corporate training function, but to describe the details I discussed the connection to a human physical. The auditor is the doctor. Evaluating only one area of a training strategy is like taking a person's blood pressure, but a physical involves looking at a lot of different areas.

This book is a continuation of the "healthy training function" discussions in my first book. I've chosen a cover for this book based on an old analogy that trainers often have used to describe limited training efforts. The bandage only works for scratches, and won't stop major bleeding. Yet in training we sometimes use a bandage solution, a quick fix for a lot of performance problems. We send people to a day of training and expect miracles.

If we look at what makes training disconnected and thus pointless, can you imagine your doctor putting a bandage on your arm that has a cut that needs stitches? It is the same if we take a 2-hour workshop to learn skills that really need two days to learn well.

When training is not supported by management or the employee it becomes pointless to implement no matter how appropriate it may be. It is a waste of time, talent and resources if learning doesn't happen.

And who wants to sign up for a medical procedure when the second opinion disagrees with the first opinion? Considering that most insurance companies will concur with the doctor, would it cause you to think again if your insurance company was also not willing to cover a procedure? I don't know about you, but I want everyone on the same page if I am going to consent to surgery.

As we continue through each skill development topic in this book I want you to remember the bandage. Ask yourself if you are applying the right solution to the problem or are you seeking a quick fix. Sometimes a quick fix is okay in a pinch, but most of the time it falls off and you are left still needing to treat the skill deficiency. You may be a trainer, but to avoid pointless training, you may need to start acting like a doctor responsible for a life.

Chapter Two
BUILDING LEADERS

How do you build a leader? There are more strategies and books on the subject, from shortcuts to lifelong processes. There are endless comments being made as to the training process and options that many give up over the shear overload of information. My goal in this chapter is to give you and your organization the information necessary to think for yourself. I want you to design solutions that work in your organization and build the competencies you need. And most important, I want you to not only avoid, but run away from pointless training options.

Defining Skill Levels

The first thing I want us all to do is broaden our definition of a leader as anyone that leads processes, functions and staff. Obviously we see the Chief Executive Officer as a leader, but in addition to others in the C-Suite, every Director, Manager, Supervisor and Team Lead take on leadership roles. No one becomes a leader overnight. Not even the entrepreneur that graduates and starts their own business and calls themselves the CEO is automatically a leader. All of us must learn not only the functional parts of the role, but the communication skills that make us leaders.

I am in the camp of learning professionals that believes it is a lifelong endeavor to learn leadership skills. Mostly because we only learn some of these skills in the classroom, and the rest of the time we are learning, changing and improving our leadership style with practice. But I also believe that these skills are like building blocks. That the same skills we want in a supervisor must exist in a manager and a senior leader. When you learn these skills is not as important as understanding that just because you carry a title, doesn't mean you get to skip the developmental phases that the title should possess.

Every person must develop the tactical and functional skills for their job. As a company, you will determine those skills based on your operation. For the purpose of our discussions in this chapter we will limit it to the communication skills needed to build leaders. Other chapters will identify current audiences that benefit from a particular skill development, and what you might want to include in succession and career plan development for leaders.

When it comes to designing training programs for building leaders, it is common to design three general phases. I break these down as Supervisor, Manager, and Leader levels.

Supervisors are seen as having the responsibility of getting things accomplished with the help of other staff members. They generally don't have the ability to hire, manage performance or terminate employment, so we are building skills that help them achieve their goals within their working parameters. Think about skills in basic communications, getting people to perform functions, giving feedback maybe even handling change and teamwork. The goal should be to introduce them to techniques and strategies for leading a workgroup. A supervisor will be developed into a manager next, so lay some foundational skills before they are promoted.

Managers are seen as having the responsibility for getting things done with the help of other staff members too, but they also have the ability to interview and hire staff. They set performance goals and objectives and must communicate them to staff members. They need to give constructive feedback to keep staff on track, and become a coach that can motivate even better performance. When employee performance needs correction, they must be able to have the conversations that include employment consequences up to and including termination. The key to management development is the ability to connect and communicate one-on-one with people. At this phase you are building skills they will use for the rest of their career.

Leaders are managers and again have the responsibility for getting things done with the help of other staff members. While most leaders have direct staff that they manage performance for, they now have other managers reporting to them. They also lead departments, divisions or like a CEO the entire company. Leaders must recognize and learn how to manage other managers, a skill set that many leaders fail to obtain and still try to micro manage everyone. They must be trained to see the bigger picture, think and design strategically and instead of just managing change, they must be able to lead change initiatives. At the point a manager becomes a leader their critical thinking skills must be well developed or entire operations can be undone by poor decisions.

The point I'm trying to make is that a manager must know how to get people to perform their jobs without resorting to using their power as a manager to force their will. And yet the same skills taught to every manager need to be firmly in place for every leader in the organization because they have individual staff performances to manage.

These are not fully comprehensive lists of skills, and as you go through the upcoming chapters you will see things like customer service, sales, interpersonal communications, presentation, meeting management, systems, operations, and productivity as additional skills that are not unique to managers and leaders, but highly sought after skills all roles can benefit from to some extent. Your job is to design and build the very best leaders for your organization.

Defining Functional Skills

Every employee in your organization deserves to know the list of functional skills they should possess to perform their job properly. When it comes to building leaders, each person must be simultaneously building functional skills with communication skills. Career plans that identify the skills by functional area help employees to see what they need to know and be able to perform in any given area.

If we break down Human Resources into core functions like Recruiting, Talent Management, Training, Benefits, Compensation, Payroll, Employee Relations and Compliance we may find someone called a generalist who can do a little of everything. They may have spent more time in one area or the other, but small HR functions usually attract the ones that can oversee multiple functions. I personally think the best HR Directors are generalists that may only need the strategy and planning side to perform well. For someone that is in training as an example, a well-developed functional skill list for that function would help people develop a career path in training. Not everyone wants to be a HR Director, but as a company you now have the list of functional skills you want developed in this leader if each of the separate functions in Human Resources is spelled out.

While this is a long and often tedious project, the time spent rarely needs more that an annual review to make sure technology or company direction hasn't changed the list of skills. The process is the same for accounting, purchasing, IT, operations, compliance and every other department.

Managers and Leaders must know how their department works. Both communication and functional skills are needed to build leaders. Skipping one or the other is preparing for disaster. Also short changing this development makes success even harder to achieve. And to clarify, when I say short changed, I am saying, both skipping skills, and not bothering to train anything at all. So many organizations pass on the communications skills at a certain level in the organization. And unfortunately, I have met a lot of senior leaders that couldn't communicate well with other employees. They cause irreparable damage at times, and their lack of skills makes it hard to perform their job well.

While most of the discussions in this book are about how to avoid pointless training solutions, not training people in skills they need is as damaging as poorly orchestrated solutions.

Learning Pattern for Development

While how we learn anything is as important as learning the right things, I am choosing to talk about how adults learn best in this chapter because it is so important to develop these skills over a period of time. Building leaders is a long process, and good leaders never stop learning. Please remember this page for all skill development as a road map to building skills that stick.

When I talk about a learning process we factor in more than what the learning modality is (a classroom workshop or a self-paced eLearning course) but rather it is a process of steps to take for learning to happen. In fact you will note that most of the time I will say "event" because I am not specifically endorsing the media type of training. A learning pattern is the process in which we develop skills.

This has been my roadmap:

1. Opening the Mind to the Concepts
2. Learning the Skill and Techniques
3. Practicing the Skill
4. Using the Skills
5. Getting Feedback
6. Training Others

Opening the mind to the concepts being trained is a way to engage the learner before the actual event. Using pre work assignments such as an introductory level eLearning course, and/or book on the subject, can be easy ways to begin the learning engagement. When the participant attends the main training event they are given the chance to learn the techniques and practice them in a safe training environment.

Practice should continue with activities performed on the job, or a simulation activity where nothing is at stake if the skill isn't performed correctly. If you are using coaches or on the job trainers, have them conduct the activity and provide feedback. If this is a new role for your coaches and on the job trainers, make sure you train them on how to perform their part of the learning process.

Allow the learner to start using the skills in real life situations where their manager can provide constructive feedback and reinforce skills that were performed well.

Lastly you will want to help individuals maintain their competencies by training others. We know that when you have reached the level of competency that allows you to train others it is well imbedded in your skill set. Sometimes it is hard to locate coaches and on the job trainers to help in the training process. However, if you plan to use your graduates from the first program to help with the next program group, you will never run out of well-trained people to coach.

I could tell you that this six step process is not necessary all the time, but I'm not going to encourage that as a practice. When it comes to building solid leaders for your organizations you don't want to take short cuts, because it is so vital that you build these skills to last. Otherwise your efforts could end up being pointless and a waste of time.

Off the Shelf or Customized

Whether to customize supervisory, management or leadership development skills is a matter of choice in some cases, and in others you are left with only the ability to create your own program. My rule of thumb is whenever I can make off-the-shelf work for my needs I do, and leave the customizing work to the areas I cannot purchase completed materials. And for the most part this is the way I approach most any skill development.

For several reasons, customized programs cost more. They cost more money to develop because the work is being performed for just your needs. And this goes for internal design and external contractors. It takes longer to begin the training process and my goal is to train people, not just prepare to train people. Some wheels don't have to be reinvented so purchase a wheel that has been vetted by a number of companies that have purchased before you.

Functional skills will be discussed throughout this book, and many times we can train concepts like accounting, financial analysis, budgeting, Microsoft Suite and business acumen using vendor programs. You may still need to customize the delivery, but the vast amount of content out there for purchase limits your need to develop everything yourself.

When it comes to communication skills, basic management and leadership development concepts, it won't be a problem finding off the shelf solutions, but it will be hard to choose which ones to purchase. As I said earlier, there are so many ideas and methods, there is bound to be a good fit for your needs.

There is a section in my first book, **The Training Physical**™ that I discuss how you work with vendors. I made a point there, and I will make it again here, you should always know what you want to train before you go shopping! Otherwise the vendor will sell you what they have and it becomes what you need.

This is why, when building any kind of training program, but especially when building leaders, have a detailed list of skills in hand. Break down the skill so you are clear what you want to train and you match it to the learning objectives in the program for sale. Don't be surprised if in the course of shopping, you do discover a missing skill set on your list. Vendors that develop this kind of training for sale have really done their homework. So take advantage of their research by comparing it to your analysis.

Although you might have a super talented instructional designer that can create a coaching module, you must ask yourself why that is better. The vendor program has been sold a number of times, and thus trained by numerous organizations. If the program had flaws in it, their customers would have told them and changes would have been made, giving you a finished product that has been well tested. Why would you want to use an internally designed program when a vendor program will work?

There has been a recent offering in the management and leadership development arena that is kind of a high-bred option between off the shelf and customizable. It is a product where you are sold the content in electronic files (Word or eLearning) and you have the ability to produce your own final product. You could print it off as it is delivered, or you can make changes. It is a very cost effective option if you feel that customization is important but you don't have the time or budget to start from scratch. These programs are sometimes a bit dated, but since changes can be made directly to the files you can update the content.

Avoiding Pointless Options

One of the most pointless training options used to build supervisors, managers and leaders is the one day miracle program. It could be one of the seminars that cover everything in a day, pouring in the knowledge and expecting results. It could be a single subject like emotional intelligence and branding it as "Leadership Development." It doesn't matter; it was a pointless training solution. You spent money and will get nothing much in return.

If you have never attended one of the multi-topic seminars offered all over the country, you really need to spend the money and feel what happens. A very good speaker, even a subject matter expert lends their talents to a program that simply covers too many topics in a short amount of time. Participants get a few questions answered, but competencies are not built. It is not part of the design, and thus it doesn't happen.

As an example I received an advertisement recently that said:

"Sharpen your skills, grow your career and get months'
worth of training poured into a 4 hour workshop!
Opportunities exist for all skill levels across the
workshops presented by seasoned practitioners."

Notice the overselling of expectations with *"grow your career"*, the vagueness of *"sharpen your skills"* and the reality of *"months' worth* of training <u>poured</u> into 4 hours." The perk is *"presented by seasoned practitioners",* but note they are not magicians. Honestly, you get what you pay for with this option. I have attended these workshops on occasion when I want a high level overview of the topics. I realize after I am finished that I have not developed the competencies to perform the role, and at best I have enough knowledge just to be dangerous.

But you don't have to send people outside the company walls to provide this kind of pointless training. I've watched training managers brag about their one day supervisor program, or their two day management development program. Very little practice and no follow up or post work assignments. Training is not and never will be a magic trick, and we need to set everyone's expectations in reality.

For those of you that don't provide any management or leadership training, at least you are not setting false expectations. You are just fooling yourself that this skill area can be skipped and all will work out on its own. Every organization has a leader that is a real pip, and I'd bet good money this person never received purposeful training to build their current skills. They learned on the job by some of the worst examples available.

Another process I've witnessed that is pointless is the annual retreat where guest speakers are brought in to "train" the management team. The hot topic of the moment is barely worth the money. I've had CEOs tell me that each year they offer a new topic for their managers. But considering that your organization might easily have 30 different topics per leader to learn, the one a year approach is a pointless one at making any dent in the total development of each person. Not to mention, rarely if ever, is there any follow up to this event, reinforcement or practice built into the learning process, so most of what was learned about fades away quickly after the event.

I read a discussion question online where a consultant was trying to locate *"high end, institutional training for executives."* I responded asking if the client had a list of competencies and skills to compare with available programs, or were they just looking for a program and would accept what they were offered. I know it was kind of a setup, but I got an honest answer when she replied *"they wanted an organization with prestige."* I realized this was going to be a pointless path and one that a training consultant was helping them achieve. They were focused on obtaining training that would provide skills, but not necessarily the ones they needed. I wished them all the best of luck with this approach. I didn't want my fingerprints anywhere near this project.

Building competent leaders to take care of the company today and make tomorrow possible is the most important set of skills you can provide your employees. Good managers and leaders make life at your company a pleasure, while poor managers and leaders can make life difficult for everyone. Spending the time, the money and the effort to build good leaders is simply a no brainer and something every company should do.

Chapter Three
PAYING IT FORWARD AND SIDEWAYS

Although the roles of a Mentor and Coach are different in their scope and responsibilities, the purpose in using other employees in the development process is powerful. Learning from people that have walked in the same path you want others to walk gives perspective, experience and value that won't come out of a workshop or online class. Yet we need to be conscience of how we make these relationships work, and how easily we can blow it and add another process to the pointless training list.

People as Development Tools

Even though I've been a training facilitator for 25 years, I know that my personal participation in the learning process is limited. The real learning occurs after the training event. The facilitator may be the first person that presents the skills and has a lot of influence over how engaged a participant becomes initially, but this engagement requires still more people to support the process of creating a behavior that sticks.

There have been times when I have intentionally encouraged massive efforts to train everyone in a topic within weeks. New processes like a new approach to customer service, or time management can be so much more powerful when everyone is learning the concepts at the same time. People share experiences and often remind their fellow employees of parts of the program. I remember when I launched a time management program that emphasized the prioritizing of tasks by assigning an A, B or C to each item. After a while it was common to hear people talking about a project and asking each other if a task was an A or a B. Informally, employees will help the learning process when they can.

Using a mentor or a coach in the learning process is a bit more formal. These people have specific roles and responsibilities in the learning of skills, and yet we often assume incorrectly that everyone knows what they need to do to mentor or coach. There is no single right process for mentoring or coaching, so we find experts try to suggest best practices to implement. I believe in some structure, mostly in the choosing of the best candidates for these roles, and some guidelines and expectations. Leaving the rest up to the pair frees up creativity and you watch who is really good at performing this kind of learning support.

I believe that first we should look at common understandings of when you call someone a mentor, and when they are called a coach. Mentors are often people that are being asked to develop the whole person in a variety of things. It could be for a job, promotion or even for long term retention. They are a subject matter expert and someone you would want to clone. However, to be a mentor you must want to share yourself and your knowledge with others. Some of the best candidates cannot and will not be good mentors because they either can't or don't want to share their wealth of knowledge. Never force someone to be in this role if they can't do it!

A coach is anyone that is willing to train others in a set of identified skills. A manager is often called upon to coach employee performance, as well as support newly acquired skills. Someone that will be doing on the job training after someone has attended a workshop is also a coach. If they are doing all the training from start to finish then they are full time on the job trainers.

Now, while both of these roles should be paired with participants that can work together, it is imperative in the mentor relationship. In any case, you may want to help the learner choose their partner in learning to make sure the right people find each other. Never force anyone into a mentor or coaching role, try to seek out volunteers. You are looking for people with what I call a "trainer's heart." This is someone who wants to help develop other people with skills they can share. Likewise, never let people locate their own mentor or coach without some kind of approval process.

I learned this error early in my retail banking career when a new hire was not formally partnered with another employee to shadow on the job. Call it Murphy's Law, but when you let people find their own partner in learning, it always seems that they find the very last person you ever wanted them to find. Has that happened to you too?

Managing the Process

Part of any program design that will include mentors and coaches in the learning process, should have specific goals, tasks and responsibilities. Goals include the overall objective with due dates. Tasks help everyone keep on the right learning path and support the program steps. And responsibilities make everyone accountable.

I learned the hard way once that you cannot assume that people understand what you want a mentor or coach to do. I had designed a very comprehensive emerging manager program that included a variety of activities after each training program that I wanted the participant's coach to help them with and I assumed they understood the tasks. Wrong! A majority of these very talented people had never had a mentor or coach before themselves so I was asking them to do things they had never experienced.

Thankfully I had a talented delivery manager that picked up on this early in the program and she quickly created a train-the-coach session. We then supported this group with monthly conference calls to enable questions, and then set up the activities for the next month. We highlighted the skills being developed and how each of them could support the learning process. Once we got going, this group of coaches was doing a great job.

Now, I mentioned that the pairing of mentors and coaches with the learner is important, it is also a good idea to check in every so often with the learner to see how this relationship is progressing. Never assume that no news is good news. You must check on and obtain feedback so the learner understands that the success of them acquiring these skills is predicated on this match working well.

Sometimes people start off working well, and because of other time commitments they can't keep up with the coaching responsibilities. That's okay, but we all need to be aware so we can find a replacement. I've also watched people jump into a mentoring or coaching project with so much initial excitement, only to find out that it is not what they thought it would be. They want out, but won't tell anyone. The earlier you can discover matches that are not working, the sooner you can fix them.

Tips To Avoid a Pointless Relationship

Some of the things that can make mentoring and coaching a pointless activity have been mentioned, but they are worth repeating to make sure they never happen in your learning environment.

I'd like to begin by saying that using mentors and coaches bring a new level to the learning process, but are not going to break the process if they are absent. If you can't do this correctly, then skip it rather than making what you are doing pointless to both parties.

Never let people choose their own relationship without training both parties. While I think it is great when someone finds their own mentor as an example, leaving the process to chance can make a great match fall apart and have little value. And this happens a lot!

If you have decided to use a mentor and/or a coach in the learning process, then you must outline, in writing, the roles and responsibilities. However, if you are not specifically using these people in the learning process, you can let people work on a learning path by themselves and be available to provide feedback on their plans.

Assuming people know how to train someone, let alone coach or mentor is a sure fire way to make this a pointless process. This is a formal learning process, so formalize it with training for both parties. Think how to be a mentor, and how to be a coach. I would even suggest that a refresher session be offered to even your most seasoned person or include them in your training of new people.

Chapter Four
INTERPERSONAL COMMUNICATIONS

Training people to communicate with each other is probably the best preventative maintenance you can provide to your organization. If people can learn to accommodate the needs of others, meeting people on their terms or at least halfway, there will be less conflict and a lot more productivity. And when your employees learn how to apply these skills with family and friends in order to communicate better, they come to work with a lot more focus. Everyone wins big when we all learn to communicate better with each other.

Choices for Skill Development

There are a lot of different choices in training vendors and programs to enhance interpersonal communications. I have seen both good and equally terrible programs. I've also seen a lot of bias in why trainers support one over the over. I too have a personal bias, but I believe it stems primarily from watching behavior changes that are developed in some programs and not in others.

Most interpersonal communication programs begin with a self-assessment. This is valuable insight for the learner, but if left as the only feedback can many times reinforce negative behaviors. If I agree with the findings, I am not apt to feel a need to change or do anything different. Especially if I also perceive that my way of getting things done works too! When you can factor in 360° feedback, especially anonymous feedback, people are at least confronted with outside observations. It doesn't mean they will automatically want to change anything, but at least there are reasons to consider changing.

So if you are going to spend time training people to understand themselves better and how to adapt and work better with others, I firmly believe it is pointless to go with a learning process that only uses a self-perception instrument. It is cheaper, but in this case I can't even say you are getting what you paid for. In many cases you could end up with employees that reinforce poor interpersonal behaviors, and training was a partner in this crime.

Now for those of you that are looking for me to start naming the names of programs that I won't endorse, it is not going to happen here in print. If I am consulting with you, I will freely give my opinions, but I will never blacklist any company.

I will share my personal bias for a program that I have seen work miracles when participants learn how to use the skills. I've been using the skills personally for over 20 years, and happen to be a Master Certified Trainer. I've also witnessed, firsthand, hundreds of people that have made a real difference in their personal and professional lives because of this program. It is referred to as Social Style Training and is offered through a company called the TRACOM Corporation. (See Appendix 2)

The program has offshoots from the core offering, such as for sales, teams, service etc. However, where the real magic occurs is when you open up the core program to your general population and let everyone communicate and share the experience together. Then if you want, you can diversify with a manager version, or a direct sales consultant version. I'll speak more about these applications in the next section of this chapter. Creating a common base for all employees allow for future reinforcement, and a common language to coach from a peer to peer and manager to staff. Heck, I've even used these skills coaching up the line with great results.

Now moving away from the TRACOM program, there are a lot of vendors that offer interpersonal communication programs that use 360° feedback. Once people feel comfortable with feedback, you can implement some dynamic leadership programs that support the culture and direction of your organization. However, my advice is that you research well and make solid choices. Don't train everything out there, but find what works best for your company.

As an example, you can assess leadership competencies and train to either the strengths or the weaknesses. While I've found strength based programs get better feedback and results, your company may be focused on it developing weaknesses instead. Sometimes you match the training to fit the company culture, and at other times you may use training to change culture.

Interpersonal Communications training is more expensive because of the research that backs up the assessments. However, when compared with fewer employee issues because communication is clearer it is often not that expensive in the end. If you can avoid one lawsuit, the training dollars paid for themselves.

Applications for Better Communications

You might be thinking like so many do, that your supervisors and managers are the target group. After all, they manage people and are coaching for more productivity. Yes this is a prime target group for interpersonal communications, but in fairness to everyone, just because the manager can communicate well, doesn't mean the staff member will return the favor. This is why I am a big fan of improving this skill set for everyone that works for your company. If employees have better interpersonal communication skills, then there is less conflict with peers, managers and it lowers the number of resignations because we are more often on the same page.

If you have customers, then service levels improve when all employees are communicating with customers better. Half of the battle with customer retention is meeting their needs, and it is so much easier with this core skill set.

I've found that if you have a sales force, especially a commissioned sales force, they are eager to obtain any edge they can have over the competition. I once trained a sales force that was top notch already, and yet they wanted that edge. I asked if it would be valuable to learn how to approach their clients in a way that would obtain greater attention. Instead of using one approach, I would show them how to create 4 approaches that they would use one per person based on style. This group of people were so open to the idea, I've never seen so many light bulbs going off over two days as they each realized why certain people where not reacting to their previous approaches. Over time, the feedback was one break through after another in building new clients using these skills.

So now we can see the application between manager to staff, peer to peer and staff to customer. It is really cool when we can improve the staff to manager, up line communication path too. After this it is easy for employees to realize the same skills apply to family and friends. Parents learn to communicate with kids better. Spouses can adapt for each other and understand specifically how small changes make a difference. Even friends have remarked about getting along better because they understand each other's needs.

Why are all these relationships worth a company spending the money to train interpersonal skills? While the working relationships may be obvious to a better working climate and overall improved service and productivity, when employees are happier at home they are less distracted and happier at work. And who gets the credit for their happiness?

Speaking of the company, there are some unique ways that should be identified where interpersonal communications are made from the company to the employee:

- When making corporate announcements, you can't help but address the needs of all employees in your verbal and written communications. Now everyone is listening because you are meeting their individual needs.

- When people are receiving rewards and recognition, you can create the right environment if you know how from a style perspective they would most like to receive even positive news. The impact is greater if you deliver the news on the recipient's terms, even if that means privately over publicly.

- When managers conduct performance discussions, they can adapt to the employee's need for details or level of emotion and obtain better results from each employee.

It really is difficult to make interpersonal communications training a pointless activity because of the many ways people can benefit from the skills. And yet if the learning process is short changed with only feedback and no application in the programs you purchase, then you can end up with wasting everyone's time. I also believe cherry picking the special employees that get this training does more harm than skipping everyone. So if you want this to end up being pointless, offer it to only a select few and watch minimal impact.

Do yourself a favor and everyone else you work with and really approach these skills correctly. Offer 360° feedback with training that provides time to understand and apply the skills. From that point on, make the language of the program part of the corporate speak to reinforce the skills continually.

Chapter Five
SALES IS A LOT MORE THAN SELLING

The second most common skill set that most companies under develop, and thus make their efforts pointless, is sales skill development. Because selling consists of more than just learning a sales cycle and handling objections, training departments allow sales managers to design a program that often will not deliver the targeted results. There are five key areas that make up core sales training, and three others that I believe take it to the next level.

The Five Core Skill Sets of Selling

Seasoned and successful sales people will tell you that selling is a collection of several competencies that all must be mastered and applied to achieve and exceed goals. Something every sales manager in every company wants to achieve with their team. Through training and consulting with many different sales teams, I have discovered five core skill sets:

1. Product Knowledge
2. Basic Sales Communications
3. Productivity
4. Operational Processes
5. Prospecting

Let's begin with **Product Knowledge**. Every time a new sales person joins your company, they must be trained in the products they will be selling. Knowing every feature and translated benefit of the products and services available to sell is an ongoing process with companies that either change or launch new products on a regular basis.

The sales representative must understand all of the competitor's products and services too, because they will be selling against them most if not all of the time. The training function should be creating comprehensive training for their products and services and ways to keep sales people current to changes. I also believe that learning how to keep track of the competition can be built into the learning process and develop a behavior of ongoing surveillance. If training creates product update events, whether it is a workshop, eLearning course or a job aide, and logs them into their Learning Management System as "required" training, it also makes tracking easier.

Basic Sales Communication Skills are at the root of any sales representative's success. While the training function may also be training a particular sales cycle at the same time, it is important to note that while communication skills are permanent, a sales cycle is subject to frequent changes.

In basic sales skills training we train participants in:

- Listening & Paraphrasing
- Questioning
- Presenting Solutions
- Handling Objections

Basic sales skills must be present and proficient in all sales representatives, and when training functions assume they exist and either skip or short change the learning process it becomes a pointless training effort. I've always encouraged training that involves a lot of practice, so try your best not to make sales training just an information dump. Incorporate a lot of role plays, for each step in your sales process.

I also believe that separating employees new to sales from experienced people allow for more practice time when first learning and a common playing field. Experienced sales representatives can actually be competitive with each other and bring out some of the best of the best practices and yet can learn in a shorter program. They can also be quite intimidating to a new sales person. Mixing new and experienced sales people in a training event will do more to shut down learning than it does to afford a chance to learn from their peers. Now, I do find pairing new people and experienced people of value, so I suggest you consider coaching relationships as a next step if everyone is open to it.

The frequency that training departments believe they must create custom programs when training basic and common sales skills is stunning. There are some solid off the shelf programs that can be customized in the delivery process with your products and services during practice. Certain wheels don't have to be recreated to provide quality care. I once asked a nurse taking my blood pressure how she learned the procedure. My curiosity came from the fact that everyone takes blood pressure the same way. She explained to me that every person is trained the same way and the technique is always repeated the same because the expectation is the same everywhere they would work. Hum, kind of like basic sales skills.

Productivity is another vital skill to sales. Time Management and a common sales tool called Customer Relationship Management (CRM) are at the essence of being productive. In Chapter 7 I will be going into some detail about time management training, so rather than repeat it here, make sure you read that chapter too.

Most CRM tools are online so they can be accessed by employees in and out of the office. They can be powerful ways to setup client information, track issues, and document where every sale is within the company's sales cycle pipeline. They can track calls, appointments and prompt tasks for following up. Productivity is more than just getting a lot of work accomplished it is about keeping promises. Having the right tools and an understanding of time management principles is what make things happen. It may seem silly to mention it, but since I have seen it a lot, using a generic process CRM and a specific company sales cycle is disconnected. Today's CRM programs allow you to match your company's sales cycle into the program. Please don't spend time training a CRM if these two processes don't match up.

Next up are the **Operational Processes** to getting a product or service sold. This means that there needs to be a comprehension of policies and procedures for each product and service, and the systems involved in the process.

Policy and Procedure manuals whether they are paper or online, can be some of the driest training imaginable. While knowing this information is vital to selling it can also change frequently. I've always said that it is not important that people have the manual memorized, but it is important that they know how to find the right answer. I once observed a training session for sales people that needed to learn an underwriting manual so they understood policies. They all had out this massive binder and the trainer was reading the book to them, and pausing with additional comments.

I watched about 10 minutes of this and nearly passed out for a lack of consciousness. It was so boring, not to mention I doubt anybody was learning a thing.

So rather than train any manual page after page, I've often engaged subject matter experts and my instructional designers into creating case studies. Then a series of questions that drive people into the manual to find the answers. This is so much more engaging, and if you can use a facilitator to debrief their answers rather than a stale old answer key, it allows for questions. This works particularly well when the answers are not really black or white, but rather gray like most underwriting can be.

Prospecting for new clients is not one of those natural inborn skills that the human DNA includes, so you must train prospecting methods that will work best in your sales environment. How do your sales representatives find brand new clients? Depending on your product or service you should start by interviewing your best sales representatives. I've found the best success is to survey all your sales people and compare activities with the results of your interviews. Given that there will be some things that work better than others, prioritize a best practices list using the results from your survey. Maybe referrals rank higher than repeat business, or cold calling is more effective than at first thought.

Prospecting sometimes involves a short training session, and other times if using a data base you might need to include some hands on training. The important point is to train what works best for your organization and don't be surprised if you need to change this material if you have different sales groups within the same company. As an example, a bank might train their branch sales people one way, and their lending people another way. If they have a call center environment it will no doubt be even another set of tasks that produce new leads. Never expect one size to fit all, or reuse an old process without verifying it will fit.

Three Skill Sets to Enhance Selling

Once you have the five core topics addressed you can work on skills that enhance selling results. I have found these to be excellent ways to take sales performance to a new high because you are engaging both the managers and the sales representatives to achieve even better performance.

These three skills are:

1. Sales Management & Coaching
2. Rewards & Recognition
3. Social Style Training for Selling Relationships

One would argue that if you are training managers (see chapter 2 Building Leaders) then you are already training them how to manage performance, coach and recognize results. But anyone that has managed a sales team will tell you, there are some distinct differences when the employee is a sales representative. Ideally managers should experience your normal management development program, and then attend sessions to come up with different strategies for sales.

Sales people need a lot of support, so please don't skip over the development of the manager. Even the best sales people if they become a sales manager need training for how to manage the sales process with different employees. They need to learn how to coach and motivate with each individual on their team. Just like we customize our approach in working with different clients, sales managers need to adjust their approach in working with different employees.

Numerous surveys have been conducted on what motivates people the most, and contrary to what most sales managers will say it is not the paycheck. Most people and especially the millennial generation working today, want to feel valued. Learning to recognize performance and reward appropriately gives people the added incentive to remain with your company and to work even harder. Managers need to again realize the one size fits all approach will not work. Getting a plaque might be a great form of reward for some staff, but not everyone on the team will be motivated by something to hang on the wall. Managers must be creative and sometimes the best way to get those creative juices flowing is in a training session with other managers.

In the last chapter I talked about Social Style training for all employees. The general course works best for everyone in your company except sales representatives. There is a Social Style course designed just for the sales relationship and it has a greater impact. While the general course concentrates on work relationships and participants see the overlap with family and friends; the sales course focuses on the client relationship and how to increase the effectiveness of their selling process using style. The participant naturally wants to focus on those relationships, but will usually then see the overlap with other workers, family and friends.

Social Style for Sales will always return on investment when it is offered to experienced sales people. Hold off this enhancement until the employee is looking for a way to improve. If trained too early, the skills get lost in the shuffle. If you wait, then the skills get applied quickly and they get used.

Example: Avoiding Pointless Sales Training

I once adverted the need for "sales training" when I was called in to provide training for a bank that was not closing enough loans. I met with the President who was adamant that his loan officers needed a refresher course. I asked what the goals where for their branches, and what was currently happening. When I discovered that not a single branch was making their goal, I smelled a different cause than a lack of sales skills. It turned out to be an operational issue. The process of putting the applications into the system was taking too long. Each branch was producing enough applications, but couldn't process them in a timely manner. So after evaluating the application process, they figured out a shorter form, retrained everyone on the process and goals were now being made. If we had run another "sales training" course, it would have been pointless in changing the outcome.

Just like training sales skills when it will make no difference in the current performance is a waste of time, I want it clear that not training all five of the core areas of sales effectiveness is also going to achieve results that are less than possible. Sales are one of those skills that earn the company the potential for significant return on investment, but only when you train everything needed.

Chapter Six
Constant Customer Service

You might think that once you learn how to provide good customer service you would never need to take another training course again. If this was so, customer service training wouldn't be part of the training agenda so regularly. Yet if it was done well, and for everyone at the same time, it might not need such a fanfare every year, but rather something less formal. If there is one area that gets a bandage when stitches are needed it is customer service training. For too many companies it is high time to train this content with purpose, and stop the annual pointless events.

Designing Service Strategy

For a lot of organizations that interact with the public, customer service is a focal point of their operation. While it may be featured in marketing and advertising it gets little attention in the strategic planning session. Companies create solid vision statements about service results, but fail to design the standards and measurement tools that everything else revolves around.

I'm not here to tell you what your customer service vision should be for your business and culture. I'm also not going to try and tell you what the standards are or how to measure results. I am going to tell you not to try and design, purchase or implement training until those items are in place, otherwise anything you train will be considered pointless.

Imagine the surgeon who is standing over the patient ready to operate, and knows he wants to keep them alive and fix a problem, but he is not sure how to go about it. Would you want him operating on you? Plowing into several rounds of customer service training without an end game clearly defined is just as pointless.

The training function needs to understand the outcomes and where training fits into the strategy. If the company has decided that they are developing a different focus on customer service than they have in previous years, training must be not only comprehensive, but build a bridge between what has been done and what is expected in the future. Training needs to provide employees with the techniques to develop new skills, and refresh what is not changing. If the training function simply purchases an off the shelf program and sells it as the training solution, it will train skills, but probably not all of the skills necessary to achieve the corporate strategy.

If there was ever a time to perform a complete training needs analysis, this is the type of training that you want to spend time with before shopping. There are a lot of solid customer service training programs and learning plans on the market and just like going to the market, if you have a skills shopping list, you can evaluate programs to check off how many of your skills are even being addressed by the program. Only after shopping for an off the shelf option, would I even consider that you spend the time and resources for customized training modules.

I was a consultant with a company that sold customer service training as one of their offerings, and the quickest sale I ever made was from a training manager that had a skills list prepared in advance. One telephone call, we compared her list of skills to the content of the six modules in the program. We were the eighth company she had called, and we were actually more than a fit. We actually had an additional two topics that she had not thought about and decided to include it. The purchase was made in a week, and she was training two weeks later.

What normally happens is the training manager is collecting content and deciding what would work best. This is only a win for the training vendor, as the training function is settling for what sounds like a fit for their company. If this is your normal process, I have to ask how effective will this be to create the right customer service focus for your organization? I realize you often are training common customer skills with a vendor program, but my issue is with what is missing from their program that your company will want the staff to know how to do. Using a vendor program is a good idea as long as it fits your learning needs and not the other way around. So take the time to develop a list of skills.

Here is a list of potential customer service skills you may want your employees to develop:

- Listening
- Open and Closed Questions
- Showing Empathy
- Service from the Customer's Point of View
- Paraphrasing
- Solving Customer Problems
- Handling Emotional Situations
- Resolution Processes and Authority Levels

Some industries will focus on customer service training every year. Banking is one particular industry that differentiates itself with service. So every year management often wants every employee to go through training. No one wants to attend the same workshops they took the year before, so the training manager goes out and finds a different one. Everyone takes the training, and then next year they repeat the cycle.

The first thing you ought to be asking yourself is why do they have to train customer service every year? I've found it is because the service levels (results) have not changed. Training steps up and agrees to train again because someone is asking for training and that makes them feel valued. Most of the time the skills are present and it is the environment that is not supportive. But it is easier to put a bandage on the problem and run another training workshop.

The issue I have with this very pointless effort is it won't matter how much is spent on the latest new and improved training program, nothing will change. It would be smarter to get a better handle on ruling out training as a solution, and stepping back into a performance consulting role and finding out why customer service is so poor. I did this with one bank and found that the employees were quite skilled in customer service, but it was not a frontline issue that caused poor feedback to management. It was actually the operations center, policies and procedures, and system errors that were causing all the disruption. Customers responded that they received poor service, closed their accounts in retaliation, and no amount of training was going to help the people in the branch turn this around. Since management was focused on the frontline people as the only cause for good or bad service, they were trying to train people that did not need training.

Training All Employees Required

One of the biggest goofs that most companies make also happened at the bank in this last example. They did a great job of training the branch service people, but they didn't take time to train anyone in the operations and support centers.

When I was a loan officer I worked for a bank that had a CEO that understood the purpose of a bank. He said that *"there are two key employee roles in this bank, the teller and the loan officer. The rest of us were hired to support their efforts."* As a loan officer, this caught my attention, but it has always stuck with me. One of these employees was the first contact for customers depositing money, and the other was the first contact for borrowing money. For a bank to stay in business, customers have to want to work with these two roles.

Years later I was facilitating a customer service program that was training every single employee in the company; from the President down. We were either providing customer service to external or internal customers. While no one will argue with this approach after thinking about it, this was very rare at the time in training customer service, and yet it was a very successful company and scored very high on customer surveys.

When you only train customer service to the front facing employee that directly interacts with a customer, you are not establishing the same focus for those that support these employees. If one employee is trying to solve a problem, and promises that *"thus and so will happen next,"* it serves no purpose if the back office operation sees this promise as optional. Yet if operations see their fellow employee as an internal customer and provide good service it will ultimately provide that the external customer is supported too.

Anyone that has flown Southwest Airlines probably has witnessed the Captain passing out peanuts. No it is not his job, but to provide good customer service all employees work together toward the common goal. This philosophy for customer service is part of the company's strategy, goals and specified expectations. So all of their employees are trained how to provide customer service; not some of them, ALL of them.

Keeping the Momentum

The reason too many companies are training customer service every year is because once they are trained everyone stands back and expects something magical to happen. Keeping the momentum of training going needs to be part of the strategic learning plan and can be accomplished in two distinct ways.

First, since customer service is something that happens every day of the year, plan to spend several months training the skills. Training every employee requires a lot of time, but if you break apart the modules in your program you can focus all employees on one topic at a time, and create some synergy in the application of the learning.

Let's say you are beginning with a module that focuses on service from the customer's point of view. In your first month or two of implementation you train all employees in this module. By the time you begin training the next module, all employees are talking about their own customer service experiences and whether expectations were met or not. You might want to create an online chat that requires everyone to share a good and a bad customer service scenario that each employee experienced outside of work. The idea is you train the concept, and then use the masses to support each other in applying the skill and bringing the training to the surface.

Each month you roll out another module with practice and application exercises to follow. You could train six half-day modules over a three day period and expect everyone to go out and make it all happen. But if you take those same six modules, spend at least 7 months in the training and practicing of the skills, you end up with a lot more bang for your buck. You allow people to take what they learned and incorporate it into their daily routines. It is a road test of each topic that eventually builds into full competencies.

The second strategy to consider is how you are going to reward and recognize outstanding service. First you need to know what you want to recognize. I suggest you start with rewarding employees seen using the skills they learned. That is great reinforcement of the training and seen as something worth trying out. This strategy should also be aligned with how you measure customer satisfaction already.

Maybe you use customer experience surveys. Match an appropriate award to the level of experience expressed by the customer. Seek out positive customer service experiences noted on social media because these are often seen by more people. If a customer writes a letter to the CEO, then the CEO should be shining a spot light on the individual.

If you measure store, branch or team service levels and you note a marked improvement during and after training, make a big deal about it. Please don't recognize only the manager, but the entire staff responsible.

Remember that the more people you recognize, the more people you have working toward the same goals.

Now it will come as no surprise that some of your employees will not want to participate in training, or change their behaviors. Much of the failure in implementing customer service training is the absence of the reverse of rewards and recognition. Managers should be ready to give constructive feedback and even formally manage performance for those that won't seek to improve their service skills. One of the more powerful messages that can be sent, and believe me this gets around the grapevine, is when a negative customer complaint reaches the CEO. If the complaint is found to be legitimate, and the CEO personally talks with the offending employee, not only does performance generally take a quick turn for the better, but this act by the CEO spreads throughout the organization quickly. It can spur some rapid onboarding by even the toughest critics of the training.

Tips to Avoid Pointless Service Training

For customer service training vendors, you need only be different than the last program a client implemented to entice most companies to try out your solutions. If ever there was a pointless annual training event it is customer service training. And that is because most companies just implement the training. They miss the opportunity to take any number of really good training programs and implement them correctly. This is why your employees leave the annual event shaking their heads and saying to each other, *"that was pointless" "there was nothing new" "why do we need to keep taking this training every year?"*

- Never implement a customer service training program without a written training strategy.

- Remember to train everyone so they learn and support each other. To keep the momentum going you need to include all employees

- Reward and recognize everyone doing well and trying different techniques

- Manage negative performance

Then next year you won't be training customer service to anyone other than brand new employees.

Chapter Seven
Continual Productivity

Being busy is not the same as being productive. When someone tells you they work more than 40 hours a week, it is probably more like they are at work more than 40 hours a week. While there are indeed jobs that require a lot of actual time to complete the work, for most people it is a lack of focus and prioritization that prevents productivity. Whether it is strategic planning, goal setting, project management or time management, there are proven techniques that can improve individual and corporate productivity. However, it only works to the maximum potential when everyone is speaking the same language.

Productivity Ground Rules

For the most part there is really not any productivity training that is pointless, because it all targets the individual's ability to become more productive. That being said, there are ways to minimize your corporate efforts to increase overall productivity.

As an example, if you offer too many options to train one element of productivity like time management, you are going to have several versions of corporate speak for common topics like planning and prioritization. This creates difficulties for individuals and managers to support and/or coach other employees. While they might be trying to discuss the same thing, their jargon might be different which creates unnecessary barriers.

Now, while I am a big supporter of everyone being trained in your time management course, having personally trained thousands of people in a well-recognized vendor program, I know without a doubt it only works for people that want to attend. It is pointless to make something like time management training a required event. All you do is send what trainers call a "hostage" to the workshop. When you offer time management training to everyone, but require people to enroll themselves, they attend in both body and spirit because they each want to be in that room.

The last point I wish to make is that anyone can improve their productivity if as we said they want to improve, and also if they get reinforcement from others. This support system works best when the manager sees and has experienced the value themselves. When I first rolled out a time management system at a bank I worked for, I insisted that either the manager participated in a workshop before their staff could or at the very least at the same time with their staff. Depending on the manager, you might want to be flexible in which way you want to encourage manager participation. If the manager is excited, have them attend alone before their staff attends. It keeps them focused best on the content and not about the reactions of other participants. However, if a manager is a little resistant to the value of time management, they often come around quickly when they see their staff becoming engaged.

So while the only thing that can make productivity training a pointless event is forcing people to attend, most of your efforts are to make productivity training something that sparks a fire in your participants. When enough employees become individually more productive, the company naturally becomes more productive too.

Productivity Concepts and Applications

Now I personally believe that all productivity skills share a common language, and it helps if you are able to obtain all of your productivity training from the same vendor as you will not have to train different terms or processes with each concept.

Let's look at the list of Productivity Concepts:

- Time Management
- Meeting Management
- Project Management
- Planning (Individual & Strategic)
- Goal Setting (Individual & Corporate)

The foundational program that everyone benefits from is Time Management, because it focuses on the individual. It also trains the core skills of planning, goal setting, and project management. In time management you are training basic concepts that get repeated in each productivity program but from a different perspective. Time Management trains participants in:

- Respect for people's time
- Planning
- Making Lists
- Keeping Notes
- Tracking Promises and Delegation of tasks to others

- Prioritizing a Task List
- How to Complete a Goal or Project

I can't begin to tell you how often participants started to bridge their understanding of time as something we share with others and that when we don't get our part of the workload completed that it affects other people. Something as basic as scheduling a meeting between two people and someone being late, not showing up or canceling at the last minute was common and caused a lack of productivity. And then someone would say, *"what about meetings that waste all sorts of time?"*

In time management we train people how to plan their day, their week and even farther out. We train how to set a goal, then how to break it down and accomplish the goal. We are essentially training individual project management when we are showing them that planning a vacation (a goal) is a project.

So while everyone benefits from the core time management course, you save your meeting management for those that actually plan and lead meetings, and your project management for those that plan and lead large scale projects. If you are using the same vendor for all three programs you are going to be able to easily transition from the individual concepts learned in time management to good meeting management and project manager responsibilities.

Productivity Hard and Soft Skills

If there is a way to make productivity training a pointless activity it is by only training either the hard skills or the soft skills. Good soft skill programs realize that they must incorporate the hard skills into their theoretical program.

Starting with time management the purpose is to give the individual both an increase in their personal productivity and a sense of balance and control over their lives. While some can read a book, or sit in a program that discusses lists, planning, goals, and prioritizing, few are able to put it all into action without some kind of system. Some will use a paper planner, while others want to work with their email software or handheld device. As you decide how to implement training, you must provide options. You might end up running three versions of your time management program; one with a paper planner being provided, another within your computer lab, or one focused just on handheld devices.

Meeting Management is mostly about the concepts, and you are encouraged to use your existing time management tools and shared systems like email to manage the tasks. However, meeting planners use a variety of planning tools to get ready for meetings, and for tracking activities and next steps that came out of the meeting.

Project Management is more of a split between understanding core concepts and then learning how to use shared software that the company has in place. Your job in training is to provide training in the current software that project managers must be able to use. Always a good idea to verify with the Project Manager Leaders that you have the right version of the software and how long they are going to use it before any expected updates. Imagine how pointless your system training would be if in another 3 months you are dragging everyone back to relearn a brand new system. In this case you might want to just negotiate a later roll out of the training.

For large project management divisions, you may find that there are several layers of competencies. Always be crystal clear about the content of the courses, so that you are not over training people. In my experience the leader of that unit already knows what each member of their team needs to learn, so make sure you don't skip this vital discussion.

By now you have probably guessed that I would have a personal favorite to recommend. Having used the Franklin Planner system for over 30 years, and I have trained 6000+ people in time management there really is no better system I have found that develops changed behavior and gives life balance back to the individual. The Franklin Covey company has a variety of Time Management programs to fit any model someone wants to use, but trains everyone in common language. They also have a dynamic Project Management program for full time project managers, and an easy to learn process for anyone that wants to learn Meeting Management. All three of these programs start with planning, then prioritization before any implementation.

Chapter Eight
PROFESSIONAL PRESENTATION

Nothing has ever caused me more anxiety than to watch a manager or executive leader struggle when they spoke. They could have been the sharpest tool in the shed, but because they lacked the skills to present themselves well they came off as a bumbling idiot. And yet presentation skills are not just formal stand up speeches. People are judged by others on how well they communicate in small gatherings, meetings, conference calls, and in all written correspondence. In this chapter we will explore what every organization should be training employees in whether it is by choice or necessity!

Selecting the Right Vendor

Choosing the right vendor program to train professional presentation skills can be a daunting task because they all profess the ability to achieve results. The truth is they all do train techniques that can improve presentation whether it is verbal or written. I have participated and trained several over the past 25 years and there is only one vendor I will recommend if you want to develop skills that will stick with people and will change the current results.

So I am going to toot the horn once again for Franklin Covey. Since this company focuses on productivity and leadership training, their Presentation Skills and Writing Skills keep those two factors in mind. These are programs that you may want to reserve for managers and leaders, or open to everyone if you are generous. It really depends on how polished you want your written and verbal communications to be in your organization.

I only recommend programs where I have directly seen the benefit of the learning beyond what has happened to me. Yet I will say that it has been 20 years since I first took these two programs and learned how to facilitate them and I still use the processes today.

Both programs begin with planning the message and answering the questions of what do you want your (reader or audience) to:

Do, Know and Feel.

Have you ever sat through a presentation, read a proposal or email and wondered if you were supposed to do something? And honestly, if someone is talking to you or writing you they want something done. Yet, more often than not they miss telling us. If you cannot identify what you want someone to do before you start to communicate, then you are probably not going to get done what needs to be done.

Then they ask participants to identify what they believe their (reader or audience) needs to know in order to act. In fact, many times we skip this step and blunder into communication without including all the vital information. If we want a decision we need to provide background and vital facts otherwise we have to play catch up for days answering questions.

Lastly and probably the most important is to identify how we want our (reader or audience) to feel. Do I want them angry, sad, empathetic, happy, anxious or excited? Depending on what will motivate them in doing what needs done, the right emotion must be included in the message and the examples we provide. It even helps us choose our words to match the desired emotion we want to achieve.

The next phases are drafting, writing, editing and practice. There are different words for each program but essentially the details to help convey the message. Both of these programs spend a day in planning the message and a second day in presenting it well. Yes, you can offer it in a day, but count on something missing from your results. Do yourself a favor and run the 2-day version and develop lasting skills.

Presentation and Facilitation

Now while the last section covered both presentation and writing, I want to focus now on only presentation and facilitation skills.

Presentation is more often than not a one way communication from the podium to the audience. Whether it is formal or informal the information flow is from one that knows something to many that need to know. You may have a key note speech to deliver or a report at a meeting.

Facilitation is usually connected to the training world and we expect our trainers / facilitators understand that adults often have a lot to contribute even in programs that provide new information and skills. The art of facilitation is that the conversation moves around the room between many people, and the leader of the group facilitates to make sure everyone stays on topic and that all of the concepts are discussed.

If you have ever led a meeting you probably have had to master both presentation and facilitation skills as they are both used frequently.

Training must recognize that most programs you purchase off the shelf only train one set of skills or the other. It is best to train the program that will provide the skills they will use most often and backfill with the differences if they need to be able to bounce back and forth. If time allows, you can add a module at the end of a program that trains the differences.

Now what you have not read because I have not written it is that you don't really learn presentation and facilitation skills completely outside a traditional instructor-led workshop. You can learn the details in an online class, but practice with feedback in a live setting is how you develop these skills.

I can't tell you how often I have watched a speech and wondered where they learned how to present. And yet, depending on the rank of the person, they probably have never received feedback. People talk about their presentation style out loud and behind their back, but not in a positive way. Those of you in training leadership would do your senior leaders a favor if you would summon up the courage and offer to coach their presentation skills. You might want to plan on most of them taking offense, but offer help just the same. I've had the most success when I have offered this coaching to an entire room of executives at the same time. This method prevents any single individual from feeling like I am targeting them, and provides a more voluntary environment that seeks help.

If you are leading a group of trainers, whether they are full time, or part time subject matter experts, train facilitation and then watch them regularly and give them feedback for improvement. This should be part of their job and expectations, not optional self-development.

The important thing to remember in presentation skills is that even the best training program only begins the process. You must include practice and ongoing coaching. Make those agreements up front, and you will make some visible changes in your leadership communications training.

Learning to Write All Over Again

So now I want us to focus on the written word. We write to communicate all the time. Here are the most common at work:

- Email
- Texting
- Tweeting
- Memos
- Letters
- Proposal
- Performance Appraisals

I titled this section "Learning to Write All Over Again" because you really need to relearn everything you were taught in school outside of grammar and spelling. In school you were taught to write in length. So many words or pages determined whether you conveyed your message well.

In business you need to get to the point and you must learn to be persuasive in the same space. Tweeting is the only written form of communication with a word limit, and so most of the rules go right out the door. Yet email and texting, which replaced a lot of memo and letter writing (not all), have somehow become electronic waste bins. Too much of the written communication we get is unread, even if it is important.

And here lies the reason for writing better and staying focused on what you want your reader to **Do, Know and Feel**. <u>You want them to read your writing!</u> Imagine what would happen if every written communication at your company was read and acted upon the first time. Kind of a scary thought isn't it?

While I was tempted to discuss proposal writing in the sales training chapter, not all sales people have to write out proposals. Yet, for large projects it is a wise idea to document all the agreed upon tasks and deliverables. As a company, you may want to train a follow up workshop to writing skills that address written communication in general with a specific proposal writing workshop. Have your participants write out actual proposals and bring them to the workshop so they can get feedback. If your company uses templates, train everyone how to complete each section and reinforce the skills taught in your original writing skills workshop.

Training people to write well also means training people to use the instrument they are writing with. You learned to print with a pencil or pen a long time ago, but now you may need to show people how to write with an email program, a phone, or your chosen word processing software. I went from a pen to a typewriter years ago, but would be out of my league today if I had stopped there. You may need to run training on software so they know how to run spell check, or bold something in a sentence.

Always remember to train both the hard skill and the soft skill when they are both needed to function. Otherwise, that great writing class won't get used and it ended up being pointless.

Chapter Nine
Nuts & Bolts & Glue

Training operations, policies and procedures are never the most exciting programs being offered and yet when they are short changed, or even skipped everything else falls apart. Without nuts and bolts and glue you can't build anything that will hold together. This is why people learn this information one way or another. The job of the training function is to make this learning process as easy and consistent as possible so people can acquire the skills.

Job Description Training

Do you remember the first week on your current job? Did you have any idea what you needed to do? You may have had an idea of the general responsibilities and have experience in the function, but probably you were waiting for someone to show you how things worked here.

Good orientation training is part of day one on the job. You have completed your new hire paperwork, learned more about the company and maybe even heard from a senior leader live or on video. While getting warmed up to the culture is a good start, often we drop people off the cliff at that point and hope they land on their feet. You started paying this employee today and yet you are going to let them free float around the place and hope they get the gist of things. All I can say to this type of process is, Pointless!

A better method would be a transition from the paperwork directly to the manager. This person needs to provide a physical orientation to the work area, which includes bathrooms, break room, and their office, cubicle or work station. If the person needs to setup their email, desk or sign on to the system, make those the next steps.

Once the new employee feels settled in, pair them up with a buddy that they can learn from and lean on. Create a checklist of items to cover, and begin giving your new hire a glimpse into what their daily routine will look like. Even though this person may not be the designated on the job trainer, you should choose the person you want your new hire to learn from otherwise they will find all by themselves, the very worst match in the office.

Some of you may have training set up for the next day, and here is where the rubber starts to hit the road. You are training them on how their work gets accomplished here. Even if this is a senior executive, they should be offered an orientation to your sign in procedures, intranet, phone, voice mail, email etc. Even if you have set up their office, show them the stock room, the photo copier (and how to use it) and anything else that could frustrate them in their initial time with the company.

Most of the time companies wait for the employee to struggle and ask questions. They assume their world is so easy to figure out, why talk about it. In an effort to not insult anyone's intelligence, we just avoid the onboarding process and hope that the new employee will figure it out in time. This is exactly why training the nuts and bolts and glue is so important. Yes, they will figure it out in time, and while they are trying to figure it out, nothing much else gets done.

So save everyone a lot of grief, and map out a checklist for everyone to go through when they get hired. Then by position, work with managers to create job specific tasks that before, during and after training can be reviewed. Don't worry if something will be covered in another setting. It is better to err on the side of repetition than allow things to slip through the cracks.

Policies and Procedures

When training these massive binders or online resources, we often make a decision to hand people a book and assume they can find what they are looking for when they need it. This is an option, but if you are going for actual understanding and compliance, then it is a pointless way of doing it.

As I mentioned in an earlier chapter, I worked for one organization that had this massive underwriting policy and procedures manual. Training consisted of the trainer and the participants turning page by page through the entire manual over 5 days reading and discussing each policy and procedure. When I first came on board as the Training Director, I observed the trainers to assess their current skills. Yet I was having a hard time not dozing off during these mind-numbing sessions of read and discuss. Once I realized that this manual had weekly updates and changes, multiple ones a month, I knew we had a two stage learning problem to fix.

First, we needed people to learn how to find information quickly. So we changed a few things in the initial training of the manual. Step one was to quickly go through the structure and the sections of the manual. This took a total of 15 minutes and everyone had now turned through the whole book. We later converted to an online version and did this same overview technique online.

Then we started training topics, and referencing the manual. Trainers and participants were now using the manual as intended. It was a reference guide and something people should get in the habit of using so they were always current. Not only was this change interactive, we had engaged wide-awake participants! When updates came out during training, we had the trainer's make copies for everyone, but required the participants to insert the new pages so they learned the updating process too. In the past the trainer was keeping the manuals updated for the training room, which removed a learning opportunity.

The next step was how to keep several thousand people up to date and aware of new or changed policies. It used to be the practice that a policy was emailed out, and everyone was on the trust system to read it and ask questions if they had any. Guess what? Not everyone read the emails, and people operated and made decisions that were not in line with the changed policy.

Having a Learning Management System (LMS) that everyone was prone to obtaining knowledge from, I convinced the operations department to leverage the system to train, test and track. They would send out their normal email, and now send it to us in training. I asked that they send us a Word version which we could cut and paste into a course template, and write us 2-3 questions with multiple choice answers that targeted the policy or procedure. We packaged up the "course" and assigned it to everyone on the email list. We gave them an allotted time to complete it, and operations could easily pull a report on anyone that had not completed it, giving them a list of people to follow up to make sure they learned the information.

By using training techniques, we were able to engage the vast amount of employees that needed to learn how to find and use the policy manual, and to ensure they all kept current. These techniques were tough to implement, but after the next audit returned very positive results, we knew that learning had occurred.

Later into my tenure, I learned that the operations department was going to test employees with over 100 specific questions about how the underwriting manual would have them do things. The results were dismal, at best. Actually, not a single person scored over 80% and these were the people processing and approving the loans. I was aghast that the idea for testing them <u>was without the manual</u>. I just about lost all my composure when I was informed that the trainers should give day long lectures on the manual. What a pointless adventure that would have been.

When I found out why this assessment was being given and why it was important to have passing scores, I suggested that we break the manual into 5 sections. I hired a contractor that was both a former credit administrator and an instructional designer to write situations that required a decision. The answers were within the manual, and it forced everyone to break open the book again. But since the answers could not always be black and white enough to create an answer key, I had the trainers conduct debrief type sessions. We uncovered topics and questions that could be interpreted differently and thus the original assessment was cleaned up to avoid gray areas.

Lastly, I convinced management that there was never an expectation that employees would memorize the manual so they should allow extra time to complete the assessment using the manual. This whole process refreshed everyone's use of the manual, talking about common situations, and finding answers. And the best news was the second round of assessment results had nearly everyone passing with 80% or better.

Chapter Ten
NEVER ENDING SYSTEMS TRAINING

There are days I don't feel that much has changed in the business world until I remember I learned to type on a typewriter and the first business machine I used was a key punch cash register. Having a pager was a cool thing to have on your belt, and the first cell phone was a challenge to even use. I will say I was lucky to learn to use a PC at the same time Windows was rolled out, so I never had to learn too many key strokes, but every company I have worked for has had a different operating system to learn. Add to the never ending upgrades, and changes in both hardware and software; training departments often wonder if they will ever catch up. The secret is, no we will not, so plan on just doing your best to keep your head above water.

Systems for Everyone

What systems training do you have to train that is pretty much available to every employee? Maybe it is Microsoft Office programs, your intranet, and your training Learning Management System (LMS). Find a way to make this training available to employees through eLearning courses.

When it comes to Microsoft Office, many top quality vendors provide basic through advanced training in each program and package it together to make it affordable to buy a large library of courses. Just like every employee will not need to start at the entry level course, not every employee will want to proceed through to the advanced level courses.

Your job in training is to:

- Purchase the courses and make them accessible
- Market to employees so they know how to enroll
- Never make them mandatory.

While purchasing and obtaining access is the easiest part, marketing can be a bit trickier. What I have found is that by not requiring this training and leaving your adult learners making the choice of what they need to learn, a lot more training actually occurs. You may want to increase the enrollments by awarding paper achievement certificates for every 5 courses a person completes as an example. In other words this is very low key selling, and it often is a lot more successful than hard pressure.

Hard pressure, making things mandatory, often result from silly things like someone "replying all" to an all employee email sent out from the CEO, and someone on the management team wants all employees to go through basic Outlook training *"so this never happens again."* I can guarantee you even if everyone took all four levels of Outlook training and passed 100%, it will happen again. So mandating this kind of training is pointless and a waste of time, as it will not change the outcomes.

Your Intranet is a custom, private system and it needs to be trained, or at least designed by your people. You cannot purchase off the shelf training for your intranet, and yet if you want them to use it, you will have to make this training mandatory. However, you can make employees want to take even mandatory training.

During new hire orientation, I would encourage a demonstration of the intranet, with a quick overview and really load up all of the features, content and resources you have available. Then notify them that they will be taking an eLearning course that will walk them through each area in more detail. If you have a major upgrade or feature changes, you can upload the changes to a separate course (for all employees to learn about the changes) and then update your core course for new hires.

With the addition of hardware like phones, tablets and other small hand held devices, you are going to have to include training on these systems. Not everyone is up to date, and even if they are, you are going to want to cover the rules around using these devices. I can remember the first

Blackberry I was handed, I went crazy trying to learn everything about it. I'm just that way when it comes to new gadgets. And yet, some people are not as into the technology and some you have to wonder if it ever leaves their possession they are so attached to it. Your challenge in training is to make the training basic enough to cover the needed features, benefits (yes you need to think of this training as selling to some) and the basic rules.

By the way, if you have GPS included on devices, I highly recommend that Human Resources has a policy in place for how that feature is to be used, if it can be disconnected and any ramifications for abuse and then train that policy!

While all of this discussion has been about training these topics, so many companies choose to let everyone fend for themselves. Just remember that pointless training is not always a dysfunctional training program it can also be pointless to provide technology as part of the work process, and then skip the training and expect everyone to use it according to plan.

Operational Systems

We could have discussed this topic in the last chapter on operations training, but I decided to separate it out because there is probably more than one operational system within your company that people need to learn, but not everyone needs to learn each system. Is your head spinning yet? If not, it will soon, and the spinning never stops!

While we have been talking about systems training that all or most of your employees need to learn, now I want you to focus on the smaller employee workgroups that operate on their own processing system. In a bank as an example, the teller works on one system, and the deposit side for new accounts is usually on a similar or sometimes a completely different system. Enter the loan departments, and consumer, small business, commercial, and home loans usually each have their own system to enter the application and a different access point to process the application. Once each loan is approved, another complete system is used for payments and servicing of the loans.

Your company has at least one operating system for human resources information like recruiting, performance, payroll and benefits. Chances are you have several types that may or may not work together. Identifying all the systems in your organizations, and the number of people that use each one is a monster project in itself. If you want a short cut, go and talk to the people in your IT department as they know about every single one of them!

Now in a perfect world you would want a training program for each operating system. However, it is very unrealistic to take the time or resources away from other projects to design all of these systems. If you take your master list, you will see the systems used by the most employees down to the least amount. It is your job to prioritize which deserve your attention first.

At the very least, you can create job aides for each system as your training solution. In many cases that will be a first and last step because the audience is well skilled and there is little need to train a lot of new people each year.

But if you have a large audience you will want to build on that job aid. Depending on the size, you may create hands on learning labs, or on the job checklists that show and test for competency. A savvy training manager that knows what the company is planning this year and next can also get in front of a wave if a merger or acquisition is coming along soon.

As an example, if everyone in your largest systems group is performing well, you may not place an emphasis on creating an in-depth systems training program. But if you knew that the company was planning or had announced a pending acquisition of another company and all of those employees needed to learn your system, this would be a good use of your time to document and design a formal training program. Sometimes mergers and acquisitions are the prompter for a lot of training that only became vital because of a pending influx of a lot of new learners.

Now that you are all caught up, someone will decide that we need to change operating systems. In the upcoming months, you will be transitioning from a system everyone knows how to use, into a brand new environment. If it is an off the shelf product from a vendor, even with a few modifications, remember to ask the vendor if they can supply you with training materials. Most, if not all, realize this is an excellent benefit they include in their product. If your company is designing a nearly custom environment, make sure that as they are building the environment with your training design team so that the training is aligned and ready to be implemented quickly. The training department will be a part of any new system rollout, so get very involved. If things go well you will get a lot of the credit, and likewise if it all implodes, guess who will get most of the blame?

Don't Forget Your IT Department

I would be remiss if I didn't make a point to remind everyone that you have an IT department with very unique systems learning needs. While all of them might be involved in your standard management development, or time management training programs, no other employee in the company will need some of the training the IT staff needs to have available.

Anyone that knows me understands that I like technology from a user's standpoint, but I get frustrated outside of that small arena. Once you get into the back office of IT, my eyes glaze over and the jargon is like a foreign language. So this is why I suggest a dual partnership be setup between the training designate in your IT department, and a preferred vendor that can provide the programs, resources and certifications needed by this group.

Start with your internal contact and find out what they need now and going forward. Once you have a complete list of skills and certifications that need to remain current, seek out a vendor and partner these two people. While it might be tempting to let these two people work everything out behind the scenes, you still want to keep the IT folks in your Learning Management System, and track their systems training right along with all of their other skill sets.

I have usually been lucky to use the same vendor I purchased Microsoft Office training programs from for my IT Department's unique needs. This means that any online courses taken at this vendor are being routed into my Learning Management System for record keeping and only individual workshops or other live events need to be manually entered for credit.

Now although I am spending less than two pages in this book on IT systems training, there is no area more important within your company because their learning needs never stop evolving. While you can train time management one time and it sticks, if you are training people on a data base server function, you can probably count on that changing in the coming months and years simply because technology never stops changing.

I marvel sometimes at how my doctor keeps track of all the prescription options available, old and new. He once said it is the largest area of medicine that keeps changing, and he is thankful for the drug company representatives that see him weekly to keep current and the endless online resources to read. Giving the IT department the attention it deserves by keeping them current, will avoid all sorts of unforeseen problems in the future.

Chapter Eleven
Better Business Acumen

The definition of business acumen is probably a little different for each type of company. I like to think of it as not only how the business works and functions at your company and location, but a wider view from the complete industry you work in. Training people on how to perform their job today is your first priority. Preparing people to expand their horizons within your company is the subject of building better business acumen.

Why Business Acumen Matters

My first career if you will was a brief stop in the retail industry, big box store. After a couple of years I moved into banking, and leveraged my retail experience into the branch environment. Yet banking is so much more than what goes on inside your local branch. And the banking industry is part of a bigger financial services industry. As I spent the next 12 years in banking, I soon realized that the more I learned about the business I was in, there were a lot more opportunities available to me.

Most industries struggle with creating careers for people and yet are completely surprised when people don't see any light at the end of the tunnel. Training is focused on the job at hand, and everything else is left up to the individual to explore. In some cases this might be a plan that works. Yet if your company is into developing people for succession planning, you must be open to climbing different ladders; maybe several different ladders over the course of a career.

For most companies that develop business acumen, it is for at least one of three primary reasons:

- Basic Industry Overview Knowledge
- Building Particular Job Function Competencies
- Succession Planning Efforts

Let's begin with the value of understanding the industry your individual job participates in today. No matter what job you currently have at your company, knowing the way in which you're industry functions, the purpose and where you fit in allows you to realize your place on the team. Business acumen at this overview level does more to eliminate silos in your company than even the best team training available. The bigger the industry and options, the wider the view for possible careers can be for the newest employee.

But handing employees a book or enrolling them in an online workshop is not the key to building business acumen. You must engage employees through conversations about what they are discovering while they are learning.

Two banks come to mind; they both used a particular resource to train business acumen. While the program was available in an online instructor led program supported by a text book resource, both banks opted to just purchase the textbook and hand it out during orientation. Yet one bank simply said this was a resource for people new to banking to help them understand how a bank worked. With this approach I have to wonder how many of these employees ever took the plastic wrap off these $100 books. While a nice gesture, it became a pointless training solution.

The other bank handed out the textbook with the plastic wrap removed. (Honestly this was a brilliant first step as people opened it immediately.) Then they handed out a reading schedule, with a set of worksheets for each chapter. The worksheet was a short way to prompt a discussion with their manager over the topic. Both the manager and the employee would sign and date the worksheet, and when all of the worksheets were completed, they were returned to training. The training department created a certificate of completion and entered it into the online training record. These extra steps engaged the new employee, refreshed the manager, and made handing out a simple business acumen textbook a purposeful learning solution.

The second use for business acumen training can be in building a particular job skill set. Let's say you have someone working as an accounts payable clerk. Their current job is paying invoices for the company. Yet they are also part of the accounting industry even though accounting is but one department at the company. Providing training in the various accounting functions will make this employee more versatile. They see themselves less in a rut, and more in control of their career. The company gets a better skilled employee that just might stay with the company longer. This can be a very positive return on the individual investment.

Since succession planning is more than developing the next CEO, many organizations have found that well rounded senior managers are more apt to support each other when they are familiar with the other functions and their responsibilities. The Chief Financial Officer doesn't need another course in financial statement analysis, but maybe they would find value in Marketing, Sales, or the broader regulatory environment. The key is to expand and explore and think outside the box.

Sources for Business Acumen

When companies start to seek business acumen training options, I will often ask a question that usually never comes up in their planning sessions.

"How much business acumen do you want to develop?"

If the answer is an overview, general or topic specific then there are sources that work best for that goal. Yet, if it is an in-depth knowledge that is being sought out then we might want to look to another source because the learning process will take longer. More than anything, I believe it is important that the training function assist in this project whether it is for the whole company or a single individual.

Colleges and Universities are going to offer more in-depth and advanced learning paths. Through tuition assistance programs, these can be very cost effective paths too, but it is also the longest development route. Unless you are targeting a single course to achieve a select set of skills, most likely you can find faster methods than a semester course. Complete degree programs will offer very comprehensive studies and even single courses can be just the solution you are seeking.

Because there are a lot of colleges and universities, with large course catalogs to thumb through, I would highly suggest a written goal and a list of objectives. If you start looking at options before you are clear on what your employee needs, before long you will be fitting the employee into a program that sounds like a fit.

Trade Associations are beginning to support a lot of learning for their industries. While they compete with **industry vendors**, they have the unique perspective of knowing every facet of the industry they support, and develop training solutions that map directly to your company's needs.

If you are trying to develop a single role, they will often have a series of solutions that build the competencies. If you want to then build a deeper understanding of the functions within your company, they will have overview options. And if you are looking for industry overviews, I have no doubt they have materials for that too.

Trade associations often have membership requirements in order to purchase materials and save money. Yet most of the time your company is probably already a member, and this training was always available and not being used.

Internal Custom Design is what, I believe, your last option is after everything else has been evaluated and you find nothing that meets your needs. Most of the time I endorse vendor materials first and custom design second because custom costs more and takes longer to create and thus delays the training. However, in some industries or proprietary companies, it may be your only option.

My only real recommendation when you do internal custom design is to hold tight to your copy writes, and if you use external design resources make sure that you have your legal department approve your contracts so that none of the created content can be used outside of your company without consent. If you have to go to this extent to create business acumen content, your competition could benefit from your work if you don't take the time to protect it.

Now while all business acumen training can be beneficial, it can easily become a pointless endeavor if allowed to be completely "self-directed learning." I am a big fan of every employee learning when and how they wish when they are paying the bill, but when the company is paying for it I believe it should be supervised.

I once ran a Training Physical™ for a company and discovered that tuition assistance was part of the training department function. While most of the time this is usually supervised by the human resources department, it seemed out of place in training. It turned out to be quite a time consuming part of the training manager's day researching, enrolling and monitoring completion rates, so I suggested that the function be changed to a pre-approval and then a reimbursement process between the employee and an expense report.

I was ready to suggest that training didn't need to take on this process, because all full time employees were eligible for tuition assistance, and human resources could handle the pre-approval part, but the training manager shared with me that she found the researching part valuable, and from a master list she had developed, often could provide options to the employee. When it came time to train some of this content on a wider scale she knew exactly which sources would work best.

In the end, we tightened up the process to save time, but left it in the hands of training as another development tool.

Chapter Twelve
ENGAGING COMPLIANCE

Everyone in training knows that before they can get much of anything else accomplished each year, they had better have their annual compliance training in place and ready to implement. In some companies, compliance training is so vital that is has to be completed before any other training can start. Compliance training is any combination of industry regulatory requirements, human resources, employment laws, safety and security. However, just because you have to train these concepts all the time, doesn't mean you can't make it engaging and applicable to the job.

Got-To-Do Training

As I have said, my earlier career was in the banking industry, and half of my training career supported financial services. So compliance training was a part of my annual learning plans, like it or not. Yet every industry has some kind of annual, regulatory training requirements. It might be your industry, or for safety and security, or even human resources. I call all of this "Got-To-Do Training" because if you want to remain in business you have to implement and complete this type of training.

But just because you have to do this training, does not mean it has to be the burden it is for so many companies and their employees. In this section I want to talk through some of the things you can do to add variety and applicability to your compliance training, and in the next section we will discuss ways to engage your learners.

The easiest way to implement, record and complete compliance training is through a self-paced eLearning platform. This is why most companies purchase their compliance training in this format. However, the best argument for eLearning is that the laws that drive compliance training are always being tweaked and a reliable training vendor is taking on the responsibility of keeping the content current. Even if the law is set to change in the middle of a calendar year, anyone that signs in to complete a course after the changes are made is getting the current information. This is often why reports are created that includes the completion date, so you can tell what version was learned. Self-paced eLearning courses all include tests, and you can set completion scores that meet your company's requirements.

Having said all of this, I personally can't stand compliance training that is delivered in this format and I'm certainly not the only employee that feels this way.

Years ago when I was working for a training vendor that supported the banking industry, I was asked if we had compliance training. Well we had the complete stock and then some, but I asked these two questions:

What is your goal for compliance training?
Are you setting out to change behaviors, or just
obtain a checkmark for the next audit?

Many times it was for the checkmark, but every once in a while I would get the answer of "both" and I knew we could design a better way of learning. Everyone needs proof that they trained people in compliance, but the laws were written to protect people from certain actions. When a company wanted to train for both goals, we had to come up with a very different plan.

Straight self-paced eLearning may sound pointless, but if the goal is just a checkmark, I'm good with that approach. Yet when people want behavior changes in their operations based on a better understanding of the laws and what the company needs to do for compliance, then the eLearning process is just the first layer. Once everyone has completed training in the best format to record completion, we can now incorporate compliance training into other events.

One of the banks I worked for regularly included compliance reviews (games) into product knowledge classes. Finally participants connected when and how certain regulations applied to their work. This is often how we can move from understanding about a rule or law and how we use that knowledge in our daily work environment. As a trainer I was better able to explain when a particular regulation applied than I ever was at reciting the rule of law. If you are going to have a law that prevents discrimination, people grasp the why behind the law when you tell them where they need to be careful not to discriminate.

You can train your managers in preventing workplace harassment online and then run them through situations that make them react and test their understanding of what harassment is and how to respond?

Although all training needs to be sold as a benefit to adult learners, compliance training because of its mandatory component is often just thrust down everyone's throat. This is why I believe that it too should be sold for the benefits it can provide the company. And whatever you do, never assume people understand the benefits.

My first job as a training director was for a bank, and in my second week on the job I learned that the Federal Regulators were about to put a hold on our ability to lend because we had not been training basic compliance, ever! Honestly, I thought I was on Candid Camera and someone was going to jump out and say "Surprise!" But the truth was that they had not been training at all and it was amazing they were still open. For the next 60-days all I was focused on was on Got-To-Do Compliance training! But it was more than just putting people through a number of eLearning courses. Since they had never done this kind of training before, we had to help people learn why we were doing it.

I can remember senior management just wanted to say it was the government forcing us as the reason. I smiled and said that was a short term explanation that just gets us through the training portion. If we wanted people to behave differently we needed everyone to understand the intent and purpose behind each regulation and when it applies. I fought for that position and won that battle, but not without a few bruises. I was new, and was trying to help this organization change, not win a popularity contest by going with the flow. Interestingly enough, I found out later that senior management had not really understood the regulations well either and so their initial push back was also from a lack of personal knowledge.

It Takes Effort to Engage Employees

So even though you have zero options to implement compliance training, I want you to believe you can make it fun and engaging.

Let's start with your choices of eLearning vendors for compliance. Please don't purchase a set of courses simply by checking off the titles. You should take a test run of all of your choices, and include some of your employees to solicit feedback as to which they liked the best. Unless it is cost prohibitive, I would also suggest you find a few different vendors because the look, feel and functionality will keep people automatically more engaged. This can be vital if your industry has a lot of compliance training to complete annually.

If there was ever a common reason that compliance training fails, it comes from purchasing a set of classes without testing it out on your office computers. Will it interact and report scores back to your Learning Management System? Are there firewalls that prevent certain features from working? Can the course even function as promised? If you are giving access to employees to complete on their handheld devices, test them too. Nothing will aggravate the already irritated employee more than having to take compliance training and it not work.

I've talked about working compliance knowledge into your other courses and workshops, and the best people to help you out with this are the trainers and instructional designers building your curriculum. They must take all of the compliance training that connects to the courses they work with so they can better place activities on compliance into the content. However, you will not be the training manager of the year when you make this a job requirement. It took one team of mine awhile to see why I wanted them to participate, but once they did I had everyone on board.

What your designers will find is that at times they can just point out when something applies, and at others it may make more sense to create a review of several laws and then launch into a practical application. I personally liked to use group games that can cover a lot of ground and get everyone involved.

Another popular way to reinforce compliance training and engage employees is to hold Question & Answer discussions; sometimes referred to as "brown bag" meetings because they are held at lunch times. Watch everyone show up if they don't need to bring their own brown bag because it includes a free lunch too. After everyone has completed an eLearning course in a particular topic, hold some of these brief sessions and open it up for questions. Do yourself a favor and have some questions prepared in advance and have people draw them out of a hat. The random nature of either approach can make it more informal and more spontaneous. I might also suggest you have your compliance officers, or human resources department field the questions. Not only are they the subject matter experts, but it allows them to gauge how well people are learning.

One company I worked with took this concept and made it an after work event. They held a Bar-B-Que in the parking lot for all employees and turned it into a giant compliance game night. Each operations team worked to gather points at learning booths, and the winning team each got a day off with pay. This particular center also had the best audit score that year, and it was because their employees did more than flip through an eLearning course, they were, instead, engaged learners.

Another particularly effective way to engage adults with compliance application is to hire a facilitator that has personal hands on experience with the laws being trained. Some of the best human resource training, employment law and harassment prevention workshops I ever attended or implemented were when they were facilitated by an employment law attorney. These folks bring real life examples to the table, and when they talk about a wage and hour class action suit that began with one part time person and escalated into a multi-million dollar judgement against the company, people take notice.

While the message of compliance is important, the messenger and the learning environment is what changes behavior. Even though you have no option but to implement compliance training, never believe it can't be engaging too.

Chapter Thirteen
PURPOSEFUL VERSUS POINTLESS

While the title of this book was designed to catch the attention of training professionals that want to run purposeful learning functions, I didn't want to belabor all of the pointless training strategies I've discovered in the last 25 years. I wanted the focus to be on how to make every training effort one that served the needs of the learner and the company. I hope as you read each chapter you were comparing your current practices with what works well, and when you fell short you realized it, and at the same time had discovered alternatives to implement.

In these next few pages I plan to summarize best practices that make training purposeful and remind us what makes our efforts pointless. My prayer for all of you is that your training from now on will never be seen as a waste of anyone's time or money.

Training Strategy and Plan

It is not too much to expect, and your company should never have to ask their training function to have a written strategy for training, and an annual project plan. Yet, in 9 out of 10 Training Physicals™ that I have performed, they are both missing. It is no wonder why the training function is struggling to make a difference.

If you are really trying to implement purposeful training for employees to experience, it is not done without some planning. And without a training strategy you are going to trip up frequently and create pointless learning events. As I said in my introduction, no one intentionally designs or implements a pointless solution, but operating without a strategy and plan is getting pretty close. But now that you know this, I fully expect these two keys to your future success will always be in place.

Can you design a pointless training strategy and equally pointless training plan? It is very possible if you design them both in a vacuum. All by yourself, even for those of you that are literally the only person in training, is a sure fire way to head in the wrong direction. So no matter what size training function you manage, always seek review and acceptance from your immediate manager, and all internal clients you support. Oh, and no verbal agreements, have them sign and date the documents.

While strategy is more the direction and purpose for the function, it does lay out goals and objectives. A good strategy will look further than the current calendar year, and especially if you are looking to develop a lot of skills, could outline goals for the next few years. The prioritization, with approximated implementation dates, helps everyone understand when something will be addressed. Often what was first conveyed as a lower priority gets bumped when it is seen as a long term goal rather than in six months. This is why you get signatures on the strategy before working on the plan.

A training plan is a big list of projects, with ultimate implementation dates, and progress goals along the way. This plan gets communicated often to staff and management. Updates and completions are documented. I often suggest an Excel spreadsheet so you can easily email it as an attachment to people. But never assume because you emailed it that it was read and understood. Translate your accomplishments from the report to presentations in person. I want you to be open to feedback, and learn to accommodate.

If you have led training before, you know that even the best plans will get interrupted. A full plate needs push back, and unless you are able to hire contract help, another project will get delayed. Don't be afraid to negotiate dates and priorities. And don't be surprised if something is important enough that money appears to hire help if two things really do need to get done at the same time.

Solid Training Needs Analysis

Before you begin any training project, do everyone a favor and perform some solid training needs analysis. I have often borrowed the familiar phrase that Stephen Covey used in his book *"10 Habits of Highly successful people"*, <u>Begin With The End In Mind</u>. I find that if you can ask that question rather early with your client, and get a tangible answer, you are going to avoid a pointless event.

> ***"What do these employees need to do after training is over that they are not doing today?"***

A good answer to this question will give you a target to aim at, and a tangible goal to achieve. If you go off and design a solution without a target you not only cannot measure success, you have no clue what to design.

Training Needs Analysis is more than just the workshop in question; it is the entire beginning to end learning process. It includes learning objectives at each stage, and if you do not have some actionable objectives, throw in the towel now. One of my all-time favorite examples of pointless learning objectives began with words like:

- Become aware of …
- Listen to …
- Hear about …
- See a demonstration of …

And as corny as this may sound, this training manager began by saying, "Participants will" instead of "Participants will be able to". In fairness, the workshop achieved his objectives, but the participants did not learn what they needed to learn because the learning was not designed to achieve skill development, and thus it was a waste of everyone's time. Managers don't send staff to training to "hear about" or "listen to" something. But if training has set this objective as the target, everyone must share in the blame for allowing it to move forward.

Engaging Learning Environment

Now, while it is the job of the instructional designer to create an engaging workshop and the facilitator's job to make the events come alive, it is the job of the training manager to create engaging learning environments. "Variety is the Spice of Life" is a good motto for training, and should be part of everything being done in training. Use a variety of vendors (with the exceptions mentioned in productivity and presentations) so that the colors, materials, visuals and activities change. I was once a part of a design team that was tasked with creating several courses under a topic banner of Management Communications. We went with the assumption that these 7 workshops could easily be attended by the same people, so we incorporated a unique checkpoint into the design process to keep things engaging. Nothing halts engagement like repetition!

Because of a time crunch to deliver all 7 modules in a short time, we assigned a single designer to each course, and another one as the team lead for reviewing content. Each designer had to outline how they were going to design their workshop prior to a brain-storming session. Each designer would talk through their design to the group and lay out their plans for the learning activities they planned to use. It went smoothly at first, but because we all had favorite activities we started to see repetition rather quickly. The idea was that the group would decide which course the activity would work best in, and came up with a different activity to replace it. After one very long day, we had 7 workshops that didn't repeat any single activity. We had designed some very unique and engaging workshops when finished.

Include Leadership in the Learning Process

One of the more challenging processes to building an engaging learning environment is to engage your leadership into the learning process. Some of these people are former trainers, and just love to train others. I knew a CEO that regularly trained a leadership workshop around mission and vision and he was outstanding. Not to mention, the participants just ate it up because this guy was giving his time to personally develop them. Calling this a Win-Win was an understatement.

But this is more often not going to be the norm to count on, so it becomes necessary to find other ways to involve leadership. Maybe you have them choose participants and nominate them for training. Obviously the person gets into the program, but the honor of telling them comes directly from the senior leader.

I once began an emerging manager program with a morning roundtable session of senior leaders and my room full of participants. I will say that the first time I ran this event it was weak, okay, nearly pointless. I found that I needed to prepare my leaders with a bit more information about what I needed them to do because as I learned too late, they had never participated in a training session in this kind of role before. I wanted to facilitate a free flowing sharing of information about how they succeeded or struggled based on their individual experience with leadership training. I wanted them to sell these new participants on why it would be worth the effort they were going to make over the next several months, and how getting trained before becoming a manager was a positive and rare opportunity.

Round two of the program was clearly a success, and ran into lunch with the leaders sticking around to talk even longer.

Use leaders to kick off sessions, or drop by and observe. If you cater lunch for programs, invite leaders to join the lunch and have them solicit feedback from participants on what they are learning to do. I always like to involve leaders passing out certificates or a corporate diploma for milestone events.

In one corporate university model I designed, I made each department head a "Dean" of their college. The dean role was not to be just symbolic, I wanted them to review and approve curriculum. Because I had customized learning paths based on the different divisions of this company, each Dean was responsible for signing off on what each level of accomplishment required. We issued AA, BA and MBA unaccredited degrees and they were often used as criteria for advancement within the division. I then would customize the diplomas with the appropriate dean signing the documents. While it made logical sense to involve the leaders in this kind of career path development, everyone had fun doing it too.

I remember one company I worked for that just hated compliance training, but when the CEO himself completed his courses, and emailed the workforce that he actually enjoyed them and found a lot of new information, I was floored at how quickly the employees completed the courses that year. Just like Magic!

Celebrate Successes

Your training team has worked hard to design and roll out a training program that, by all indications, has been a smashing success. Throw a celebration party and acknowledge the good work and reinforce that sticking to the purpose of this function makes for good business. It is even better when you can get the line function to recognize your efforts and they are the ones that throw the party for you. The simple idea is, that taking the time to celebrate brings focus back to the end goal, the reason you launched this training initiative in the first place. Employees are now able to do what is necessary to achieve a company objective and training had a big part of that success.

Then there is the regular celebration of individual success. It could be a certificate they can hang on the wall, a plaque or trophy for larger successes, or even graduations for long term efforts. People like recognition and celebrating successes will go a long way in promoting similar behavior in the future. When staff is celebrating a work anniversary, you may want to read off a list of their contributions over the past year. Not only will this demonstrate how much this person has done, it can also motivate the other team members to work harder.

We have all heard horror stories of recognition that is done so poorly that it has a negative effect. I once watched a manager trying to award an employee for a series of training accomplishments and was completely clueless as to what this was all about. A positive event can become completely pointless if everyone is not on the same page.

Speakers, leaders congratulating and awarding employees, need a full background. If you have an audience, they should have an overview available to them of the event. The first time we graduated a class of emerging managers we designed the program handout with everyone's name and included all of the courses, books, and projects they completed. Yet it didn't stop a manager from standing up to "toast" the graduating class on accomplishing something that didn't exist. The following graduation we included a summary of the selection process, the purpose of the training, and the expected results before listing all the work. Bingo! We had provided enough information this time to prevent anyone from saying something that would embarrass them in front of their peers, and made it an even more purposeful celebration.

Communicate Often

If there is an area we can never get good enough in to demonstrate a training function that is targeting purposeful solutions, it would be communicating. We must over communicate, and we must control the communication. Otherwise the wrong interpretations take hold, the rumor mill runs amok and before long nothing makes any sense.

I like newsletters. Generated newsletters from the training department on current progress on an upcoming program, successes that have happened, and answering questions as to why anything is happening gives control to the messenger. The more you have going on, the more often you communicate. If you feature people in print, (even if it is actually online, or a PDF document that is emailed) you get people to read it. Features about the training staff, what they are working on and quotes about the process, educate employees on the purpose of training.

I once used the newsletter tool and wrote a feature each time called the Chief Learning Officer Corner. It was my opportunity to squash rumors, clarify facts, and redirect attention. Yes this is all about marketing, and it can sometimes be the difference between a pointless or purposeful impression of employee of training.

As an example, when California started requiring all managers to attend Harassment Prevention training, they also mandated a two-hour minimum. Whether it was classroom or eLearning, the content needed to last two hours. Since we had never delivered content with a required minimum time allotment, I knew the moans and groans were going to be widespread the first day the training began. So, I launched a preemptive attack and we warned everyone to plan on 2 hours at a minimum so we would be complying with state law. A few people still complained, but most were prepared to just get comfortable and not expect an early release. But since this company was probably one of the reasons the state mandated this training (a lot of serial harassers), with the help of human resources we led with some of our own statistics for harassment complaints, and the dollar costs to the company. It now became clear that we needed this training. It also made a solid impression when this message came from the HR Director instead of me this time.

This brings me to the last point I want to mention about communicating. Include people outside of training to spread the word. When something is required by a regulator and will include all employees, have your CEO convey the message. Encouraging others to speak on the behalf of training adds credibility to your work.

Measure Results and Be Accountable

Measuring the results of a training process is not difficult if you have nailed down the purpose of training in the first place. Remember that I said we should always understand specifically what is it that the participants are supposed to be able to do after training is completed? That goal is also what we measure after training is over and our success is matched to how closely we achieved this goal.

Always be careful not to take 100% credit that just training made the performance change a reality. People often ask me why I am hesitant to take all the credit, and it is a two-fold answer. First and foremost it is never just the training event that accomplished the goal and we must share the credit with a multitude of other partners. Second, if things didn't go right, you can share the fault with others if you are used to sharing the credit. If you are always hogging all the credit you get to take all the blame for when things don't work out.

Yet I want to make it clear I believe in being accountable for when things don't work out as planned. Share the blame or take full credit for the blame depending on the circumstances, but be honest in your assessment.

If you regularly assess results, it makes for an easy end of the year recap of what was accomplished. I used to have a year-end PowerPoint easily accessible through a shortcut off my desktop. Each slide was simply "project name" and then the "results." Not only was it easy to slap together a very complete recap presentation each year, but it kept me focused on results. "We trained this, and as a result we now have this" over and over again. It was an ever present tool to remind me that all training needed to have a purpose. If I couldn't achieve a positive result, then training would have been pointless.

Problem Solver / Preventer Mentality

You have a dual role in training. You are the group that prepares employees to achieve results and you fill in the gaps when things are not going as planned. You will always be living in a reactive and proactive world.

Yet when I say problem solver and problem preventer mentality, I need to stress this means that training will not always be the solution. To be seen as a function with purpose, does not mean you position training as the solution all the time. Since your world is all about performance improvement, you need to learn when and where training works and only suggest it when appropriate.

If you come across with a training fix for every situation, then you might as well run around with a box of bandages. You are pointless to the operation, and worse, when training really is the right solution, no one takes you seriously because you always say training is applicable.

If ever there was a connection between the medical doctor and the training manager it is in problem solving and problem preventer. Yet if your doctor prescribed a pain killer for every health condition you have, would they be the best person to keep you alive? As the training director, you have a lot of tools to improve performance, but if all you do is prescribe a workshop, the health of your organization is at risk.

Some of the most pivotal moments I've had with management and knowing my credibility was reestablished, came when I was called to solve a performance problem and I offered something other than training. Becoming good at performance consulting and organizational development is key to your personal and departmental success.

The preventer mentality requires you to think in the future more than others seem to think is necessary. When an idea emerges, you may be the only person that is thinking about ramifications. But that is your job if you are trying to prevent problems and ensuring a smooth rollout. Questioning a process and what will happen if we change something, allow people to see future problems before they become actual problems. While you may sometimes be seen as the anchor holding people back, you may also be saving the ship from sinking someday. It is not popular work, but it is important and purposeful work.

Choose Learning Methods with Purpose

I have not spent a lot of time in this book talking about the learning methods that should be used in training events. By this I mean the following:

- Instructor-Led Classroom
- Instructor-led Online (webinars)
- Self-Paced eLearning
- Video
- Simulations
- Collaboration Environments
- Online Resources and Tools
- Books

My thought is that training leaders and instructional designers must take into account a lot of variables when deciding the best way a skill should be learned. Sometimes an online environment works well to disseminate information, where other times an in-person environment works best.

Then there are the logistical reasons for choosing one method over another. How many employees need to be trained? How geographically dispersed is our learning population? How quickly does everyone need to be completed with training?

If you read articles in magazines, or from online sources, you may start to wonder if you are current in the way you train employees. I think it is good to question your direction, and be open to changing if it will improve the learning process in your company. But if you want to deliver the latest and greatest just because it is available, you may not be getting a return on that investment.

Social Learning and collaborative online environments are becoming very popular, especially when we learn that the latest generation entering the workforce, the Z generation, has grown up looking to the internet to learn about almost everything. So does this mean we just leave everything to self-directed learning? Does everything now need to be video based learning? Must we communicate in only short bites of information? No it does not! But it does mean that using only one method for learning is never the best path to take for any organization.

Just like choosing the wrong curriculum can make training pointless, choosing the wrong delivery method can be too. Your job is to fully understand why we use each method, and when it fits. While it may be cool to train using a webinar, does it make sense if your entire company works out of one building? Maybe, but you must decide if it does and why.

Never Be Pointless – Always Have Purpose

If you are now serious about never leaving the impression of your training events as anything but something of purpose, I challenge you to insert another question on your Level One Evaluations:

> *"On a scale of 1-10, with 1 being a total waste of your time, and 10 being the best use of your time today, How would you rate this program?"*

Although scary, it might allow you to make a course correction early if you dared to collect this kind of feedback early.

I recently discovered a semi-pointless training solution that although began as a purposeful solution, turned in a different path because it wasn't monitored.

This company was training all managers in required workplace harassment prevention training, but they had not trained new managers that were hired after training was over. They also were running under the assumption that training had been offered to a supervisor level employee, and it had not. When harassment charges were leveled at a manager, it became apparent that the company lacked a defensive position of trying to prevent workplace harassment because too many people were not getting trained. Now the dollar cost of this settlement went up because they didn't want to lose in court.

When we start out with a purpose to provide training to the right people, but we don't monitor and review our training expectations, we end up with a pointless effort for those that didn't get trained. I'd like to offer the following comparison chart as an easy reference.

Now while my definitions in the chart below for pointless training are a little sarcastic, you do need to be conscience of what you are really saying when you choose a pointless training option.

Training with Purpose	Pointless Training
Have a written training strategy	Make training reactive to the moment
Have a written and prioritized annual training plan	Work on everything at the same time
Communicate plan updates to management team	Answer questions and provide updates as requested
Begin every project with training needs analysis	N/A - Training can cure anything
Create engaging learning environments	People need to engage themselves if needed
Include Leadership in the learning process	Never include leaders, they are not real trainers
Celebrate all of your successes of any size importance	Not important to celebrate. Training is our job
Communicate training efforts on an ongoing basis	Not needed, employees already know what training is doing

Measure training results	Measure only when it makes training look good
Be accountable for training results	Take credit for positive results
Have a problem solver mentality	Wait until someone tells you about a problem
Have a problem preventer mentality	Too much work to prevent issues from happening

For people that think everyone can run a training function, and especially those that drop this responsibility on the backs of their over worked Human Resource Directors to accomplish in their free time, I feel pity for them all. Training is both an art and a science to make it work correctly. For companies that have more problems than they have successes, I urge them to evaluate their training processes. I'd bet they are neglecting the learning function, and have under skilled people managing the function. And honestly, if you implement training in your company incorrectly it is not only a pointless, worthless waste of time; it is supporting your ultimate demise.

I hope that if anything I have encouraged you to challenge your own implementation of training solutions and that you work on improving everything you do. Your job is vital to the success of your company, and learning to do it correctly not only makes you a better training professional, every company that employs you can benefit from training that has purpose.

In my career in training I have always shuddered when I have heard someone walk out of training and say out loud it was a waste of their time. My personal goal, as I hope it will be for you too, is to never allow a pointless training event to ever occur under your watch.

If you ever need support in your efforts to provide purposeful training, please contact me.

Appendix 1: Training Topic Checklist

This is what I call my essentials training checklist. Notice I said "my" not "yours" so use this as a starter and customize it for your company.

- ✓ **Supervisory Development**
    - ☐ Interpersonal Communications
    - ☐ Team Dynamics
    - ☐ Managing Change

- ✓ **Management Development**
    - ☐ Behavioral Interviewing
    - ☐ Setting Performance Expectations
    - ☐ Giving Performance Feedback
    - ☐ Coaching Performance
    - ☐ Corrective Actions
    - ☐ Performance Evaluations
    - ☐ Basic Business Acumen

- ✓ **Leadership Development**
    - ☐ Setting Vision and Mission
    - ☐ Critical Thinking
    - ☐ Designing Strategic Plans
    - ☐ Managing Managers

- ☐ Leading Change Initiatives
- ☐ Advanced Business Acumen

✓ **Interpersonal Communications – Social Style**

✓ **Customer Service Development**

✓ **Sales Development**

- ☐ Product Knowledge
- ☐ Basic Sales Cycle Skills
- ☐ Time Management
- ☐ Operational Systems & Policies
- ☐ Prospecting
- ☐ Sales Management
- ☐ Social Style for Sales Relationships

✓ **Productivity Development**

- ☐ Time Management
- ☐ Meeting Management
- ☐ Project Management

✓ **Presentation Development**

- ☐ Formal Presentations
- ☐ Facilitation
- ☐ Writing

✓ **Functional Job Skill Development**

✓ **IT and Systems Development**

✓ **Regulatory Compliance Development**

Appendix 2: Recommended Resources

Franklin Covey - www.franklincovey.com

[Productivity – Presentation – Writing – Leadership Development]

MHI Global - www.mhiglobal.com

[Management Development – Customer Service – Leadership – Sales]

NetSpeed Learning Solutions - www.netspeedlearning.com

[Management Development – Customer Service – Virtual Learning]

New Horizons Computer Learning Centers -www.newhorizons.com

[Systems and IT Certifications]

The Telephone Doctor - www.telephonedoctor.com

[Customer Service]

TRACOM - www.tracomcorp.com

[Social Style – Interpersonal, Managers, Teams, Sales]

Zenger/Folkman - www.zengerfolkman.com

[Leadership Development]

About The Author

In 1990 Jim Hopkins transitioned from a retail banking career into the world of learning development. Beginning as a facilitator he latched onto his new found profession as work he had been seeking for a long time. *"Nothing is as rewarding as watching the eyes light up when someone learns"* is one of the many attributes Jim believes is part of a *"Trainers Heart."*

As this profession seemed a part of Jim's natural DNA, it made perfect sense to learn instructional design, performance consulting and organizational development. Using a previous management background, he was able to lead teams of facilitators, designers and other consultants before accepting a role as a Training Director and then Chief Learning Officer.

In 2005 Jim launched a new chapter as an independent training consultant, and in 2010 published his first book about a process he designed called a **Training Physical™**. Since then it has been his mission to help Diagnose, Treat and Cure training functions. He has built and repaired training departments in many different industries, putting companies on a path where training is returning on the investment being made.

Now while he has maintained a weekly blog for The Training Physical, he has also maintained a weekly blog for his company JK Hopkins Consulting to discuss workplace issues, organizational development, management and leadership development and good old customer service. These issues are often ignored so long that they create unnecessary issues for companies.

Jim has been a judge for the past 3 years for the CLO Media Learning Elite Awards, and is a sought after expert in the learning development field. He is always looking for new challenges and serious business connections. He invites you to connect with him if you have a question, or an issue you think he can help you with. The first consultation is always free, so reach out today!

JK Hopkins Consulting – www.JKHopkinsConsulting.com

The Training Physical – www.TheTrainingPhysical.com

Jim's LinkedIn Profile – www.linkedin.com/in/jimhopkins

JK Hopkins Consulting's BLOG - https://jkhopkinsconsulting.wordpress.com/

The Training Physical's BLOG - https://thetrainingphysical.wordpress.com/